BPD FROM THE HUSBAND'S POV

*The Roses and Rage
of My Wife's
Borderline Personality
Disorder*

ROBERT PAGE

Book #2 in the *Roses and Rage BPD* Series

Copyright © 2019

For more information, visit the Amazon Author Central for Robert Page at
amazon.com/author/robertpagewriter
or email: robertpagewriter@gmail.com
And join the Facebook support group: Roses and Rage: Spouses of Borderline Personality Disorder

Print version ISBN-13 9781702625340

And if the band you're in starts playing different tunes,
I'll see you on the dark side of the moon
--from "Brain Damage" by Pink Floyd

CONTENTS

INTRODUCTION

"I'll suck your cock if you help me pay bail."

The red-headed woman I had never met before made her offer without any pretense or emotional attachment. She was simply stating an opening offer to a negotiation. She would deliver X if I would deliver Y.

And now she sat waiting for my acceptance or counter offer. Something like, "Okay, but you gotta wash my car too. There's been a crap-load of sap dripping from the Sweet Gum trees lately."

Instead, I quietly moved to a different row of chairs while she looked for another potential business partner. I would never be able to get it up for her anyway. Any memory of the place I was in would hardly be a turn on.

I had been at the sheriff's county lockup since 10 p.m. the previous night. Ginger's proposition occurred around 3 am. It had already been a damn long night and I was sure to still be up at dawn.

The evening had begun with cops knocking on my door. Statements were taken. Wrists were cuffed. The squad car was driven. The suspect (me) was handed over for processing.

"Years of education?"

"What?" I asked, being overwhelmed by the blur of unfamiliar sounds, sights, and smells. Everything reeked of vomit, body odor, and not quite enough disinfectant.

"Years of education sweetie?" Proof I was in the South. Even the lady at the sheriff's office calls suspects "sweetie."

In the windowless florescent lighting of my sterile surroundings, everything took on a hazy pallor. I imagine the time of day never changes in that room. It is always processing time, with the same series of questions. Name. Address. Prior convictions. And the pressing request of the moment: years of education.

I focused hard on my inquisitor's soon-to-be-forgotten face and was able to cobble together a few words despite my increasing confusion. "All of them," I said with dry sincerity.

What brought me to this new low in my supposedly routine middle-class existence? What circumstance delivered this wonderland of fresh hell? One thing only: and the worst cliché of them all—the love of a woman. God, I'm pathetic.

Around 4 a.m., a group of us from the holding area were herded down a hall to face the night-court judge. When my turn arrived, he looked over some paperwork and without raising his head declared, "You're charged with felony domestic abuse. You are not allowed to have any contact with your wife until the trial date. Make arrangements to have your personal items removed from your house."

"But Your Honor," I broke in. "How can I make arrangements if I'm not allowed to..." "NEXT" he shouted as I was shuttled out the side door.

Pathetic.

To the right of the payphone back in the holding area was a list of bail bondsmen that could be called 24/7. I picked a number, called my 5 a.m. savior, worked out the details for him to pick me up, and gave Ginger a shrug as I headed for the door. She flipped me off.

PA-THE-TIC.

♦ ♦ ♦

I'll return to that night later. For now, I wish I could tell you it was an anomaly, but the jailhouse experience would eventually be just another mile marker on the bat-shit crazy highway known as **borderline personality disorder**. (Note: when referring to the disorder, I use lower case. When referring to a specific person, I'll capitalize, as in "Borderline" or simply BP)

Since you're reading this, it's a highway you're probably familiar with.

On this road, all directional logic and previous driving experience are suspended. The offramps are either not marked or completely mislabeled. Speed limits are somewhere between full-stop and warp ten-and-one-holy-half-fuck-what-just-happened? Meanwhile, the weather shifts from mild to catastrophic in the time it takes to say, "I have to leave now" (words I eventually learned to avoid).

It was all because I had unknowingly married a Borderline. I'd never even heard of the term until a couple years into our marriage.

"Borderline." What a shitty name. It suggests that the problem is not quite a real thing. "Yup, someday it might be a *real* personality disorder, but you're in luck! It's only on the border."

BPD is definitely a full-blown disorder and I would soon learn more about it than I ever wanted to. It came to define every moment of our lives and took on a life of its own. Soon, the beast in the room earned a proper name and I began to simply call it "the Crazy."

The label has stuck over the years, even though I know it's insensitive to those with BPD. Screw it. The Crazy tried to destroy lives. Me being somewhat gruff about the attempt seems an acceptable response.

I'm not mad at the person with BPD. She wasn't the one trying to implode our world. That's all been worked out. But I don't have any sympathy for the Crazy. We are not friends.

Separating my wife from her actions by assigning them to the Crazy may not fit into the progressive view of avoiding negative labels, but it's how I cope. I'm sure there are thousands of BPD spouses out there who get it, and I offer no apologies.

I spent most of those early years assuming I was doing MANY things wrong. I would agonize over the presumed problems and their supposed solutions:

--"My poor wife is so upset; it's my job as a husband to rescue her and make it better."

--"Yeah, if I could just solve the riddles, I'll be her hero and everything will be okay."

--"I'm a smart guy...there must be *something* I'm not doing right."

--"She'll eventually realize there are better ways to deal with her feelings."

--"I'll just try harder to explain my thoughts to her logically. I'm sure that will make a difference."

Oh man, I had a lot to learn. And the lessons would often come with devastating costs.

Friendly fire is as wounding as any other kind, perhaps more so because it's coming at your back.

My Pre-Marriage Backstory

By most accounts, including my own, I was once just an easy-going American Dude. I enjoyed rock music, drank dark beer, dug fast cars with 8 cylinders, picked up the dog crap on Sundays, liked grilling burgers, grew up with a loving family, went to college, made a living, went to more college, and made a better living.

There had been many romantic relationships along the way. Some lasted years, some only a short weekend in Tijuana. But whatever the length, I don't think it would be a stretch to say my partners usually thought of me as mellow.

Hell, people had been referring to me as "cool" since I was 12. By 14, I knew the lyrics to every song on "The Wall" from Pink Floyd. At 18, my drink of choice was unsweetened sun tea. As a 20-year-old, my favorite hallucinogen was listening to "Bitches Brew" from Miles Davis. That's pretty damn mellow.

I had never had a fist fight with anyone outside of my siblings (and all siblings out there know those don't count). I had never been in a shouting match with a girlfriend. I had certainly never raised a hand against a woman.

Of course, I had never done those things. That's the kind of stuff losers do who end up on unscripted cable television, right? Not run-of-the-mill, well-educated dudes like me.

It was exactly those kinds of mellow attributes that first attracted a certain young, talented, and adorable college student to me. Lyssa (not her real name) had been enrolled in a class I taught the semester I completed my doctorate degree.

I can hear the judgement now: "He dated a student? What a dope." "He should have known better."

Yes, I did.

Yes, I was.

And yes, I should have.

But it all seemed perfectly charming and above-board at the time. It wasn't so long ago that such relationships were practically expected of male professors, so take it down a notch and let me continue.

Our first date was in the last two weeks of school and she had already locked up an A+ with her stellar work throughout the semester. My dissertation was successfully defended, manuscript submitted for printing, and I had a fulltime position as an assistant professor waiting for me in the fall.

Lyssa and I had recently worked on a school project of mine outside the classroom and as it concluded, she boldly let me know she'd like to "go on a date" sometime and continue getting to know each other.

I revealed her romantic overture to a colleague who very calmly said, "She's a cute girl and you've worked hard this year, so have a little fun. You *deserve* this."

He was right! I needed to cavort and carry on a bit to celebrate my recent accomplishments. And she came along as a willing partner at just the right time.

Lyssa's Backstory

Lyssa was 16 years younger than me and only 21 years old when we met, and I loved that about her. It was refreshing to view so many of life's details through youthful eyes.

I had never met a person with more book smarts. A true intellect. And she wasn't a one-topic fluke. She was academically brilliant in all subjects. Any task assigned to her in the sciences or humanities was completed accurately and on time. For her, any grade less than "A" was a personal failure.

The second-oldest of eight, her siblings were home schooled and lived a rather sequestered life. They made their own clothes, canned fruits and vegetables, ground wheat into flour for baking, read books from an enormous family library, had no TVs, radios, or personal phones available in the house, and computer/internet time was rigidly supervised. Most of their social interaction revolved around immediate family and church.

To visit her family was like seeing the Brady Bunch living in the Little House on the Prairie; two groovy parents with a passel of well-groomed, dutiful kids. I would later learn the darker reality.

Lyssa was quite a catch during that first summer we dated. Soon enough, she was basically living with me. She could bake pies from scratch, hold her own at Scrabble, inspire great conversation, and fuck like a motivated escapee from the nunnery. A pretty solid skill set.

Our Life Together Begins

By August, I was set to leave for my new job in the Old South. Lyssa and I had been having such a fun summer that I invited her to move with me and have a life together. She swiftly agreed, and we put our plans into action.

Within a couple weeks, we loaded up a U-Haul, grabbed the cat, and hit I-40 going east.

Life was good. I had finished a doctorate degree in a wicked-fast 2 years, 4 months, and 3 weeks. A tenure-track job awaited me (this was during a financial downturn when such jobs were scarce). And I had a young cutie to keep it all interesting.

I was golden, baby! What could possibly go wrong?

Most. Every. Fucking. Thing.

Cosmic karma wields an enormously punishing hammer, and it would soon be making regular contact with my thick head.

But for that summer, I remained an innocent in love, and life was indeed good.

I would also like to take a moment to express some of the many ways Lyssa was a fabulous person to befriend at the time. As my narrative progresses, you might infer that the tone is decidedly anti-Lyssa, so I think it's important to present some balance and perspective going in. You see, of the various goals I have for this book, none of them are to trash her humanity.

As I hope you will come to understand, nearly all of the deplorable behavior between us was nothing she pre-conceived. She was not an evil person out to get me or anyone else. If you get struck by a bolt of lightning, you don't accuse it of personally hunting you down. It's just doing what lightning does without regard for personality.

When I first got to know Lyssa, she was a charming, witty, humorous, and creative soul with downhome country cuteness in her naturally rosy complexion. She had a smallish button nose and a liberal dash of freckles that cheerfully announced, "Adorableness coming through!"

She was caring, intuitively aware of my moods, quick to offer a shoulder rub, enjoyed a good laugh, easy going when it came to hanging out, and (as I learned a little later) was an excellent housemate to share space with.

Were there any blemishes on this pretty picture I'm painting? Yes, a few. But nothing that wouldn't be seen in any budding relationship. Only with 20/20 hindsight did they stand out as early warnings.

I (and you) may question the thousands of times I chose to tolerate behavior that came later, but I offer no excuses for being attracted to Lyssa in the first place. I was as smitten as she was delightful.

◆ ◆ ◆

Why This Book?
I have two groups of readers in mind for this book.

First, and this is probably the smaller group, are those who have symptoms of BPD. If that's you, there are many excellent books and resources available regarding analysis and treatment. There are also an ample number of first-person accounts from those who have been diagnosed with BPD. I list some in the last chapter and suggest you check them out if you haven't.

But there is a gaping hole when it comes to first-person accounts from the people hardest hit by BPD who don't actually have it. If you want to upturn that information desert and gain intimate understanding of how your spouse views and reacts to your BPD behavior, this is the book for you. You may find it one-sided, but that doesn't make it invalid.

It took me years to grapple with the concept that most of my wife's bizarre actions were beyond her control. She was not able to make any other decision at the time other than the one that was usually the most counterintuitive and destructive. At her worst, the BPD was in a position of absolute dominance over her.

I suspect you will see yourself in many of the personal accounts I share here. And maybe knowing what those scenes look like from an external point of view will be enlightening and helpful.

Or perhaps, like my wife at the time, you'll be convinced that I am both an angel of grace and a devil of abuse. You will be torn between trusting me entirely or dismissing me outright. I get it. You're not comfortable with grey areas.

Regardless, I wish you well and sincerely hope this book helps.

The second group of readers for this book, and the ones more likely to be reading it because of the title, are the husbands of those with BPD.

I believe that, like me, most the spouses of BPD don't realize for a substantial length of time that they are, in fact, spouses of BPD. We typically don't have the background required to identify such issues, even if they are right in front of us. We only become aware after an arduous series of unsure baby steps and painful revelations.

The Crazy is crafty that way. It hides in the shadows and is a brilliant mimic and ventriloquist.

With nearly imperceptible deftness, the Crazy will cut you off from family and friends, isolate you from outside influence, make you doubt your established worldview, convince you to abandon core principles, and ultimately accuse you of all the misdeeds that in reality are being done *to* you, not *by* you.

Most spouses of BPD are truly unprepared to handle such a brilliant and comprehensive onslaught. A non-BP (spouse, immediate family, lover, close friend, or workmate of a BP) will likely go years making all the same misinformed assumptions I did: "I can figure out how to make her happy and solve her problems. I just have to try harder."

Lyssa had even made me promise to her during the first year of marriage that we would never discuss any of our disagreements with anyone else.

At the time, that sounded like a reasonable concept—*respecting your spouse by not trashing him/her to others.* What loving husband among us wouldn't quickly agree? Much later, I learned it was nothing more than the Crazy asserting control and keeping me from learning the truth about BPD.

If I never talked to anyone about how weird things get, it wouldn't seem so weird. Heck, maybe it's just the normal way new marriages go as two people combine their lives. "Nothing to look at here folks; just a regular marriage with a couple minor hiccups."

It's all deception of course. But I didn't know it until I had suffered countless life-threatening events, acts of physical violence, horrific emotional abuse, and the occasional visit from the afore-mentioned neighborhood sheriff.

Another devastating outcome of BPD is the thousands of dollars in expenses resulting from lost days at work, repairing or replacing destroyed items, counseling, medical treatment, medications, moving out, moving back in, forfeited apartment deposits, court fees, fines, lawyers, and the list goes on.

And even in the thick of all these events, I wasn't sure of the core problem. I just couldn't wrap my head around the concept of BPD when it was first presented to me.

I dismissed what should have been indisputable evidence. Repeatedly, I concluded, "Even if the problem has something to do with that BPD stuff, I'll solve the mystery and give us the loving marriage we both dream of. It will just take some more time. I can fix this." Sound familiar?

So, this book is primarily for you spouses out there who are confronting your own version of the Crazy. I'm talking to you directly and with no secret agenda or vendetta. I'm just a lightning bolt of BPD information. Ain't' nothing personal, baby. Are you ready to listen?

I want you to know that what you're facing *has a name*. You *can* find answers. You *can* rediscover a path to calm.

As a reader of this book, you are already close to knowing the truth. It's getting harder for you to deny. What you're facing isn't normal. It isn't your doing. And it definitely isn't how love should feel.

Perhaps, you'll learn that the questions you've been asking were based on bad intel. You'll awaken from the haze. You'll educate yourself. You'll find power in your new knowledge. You'll take steps you didn't think were possible. You'll become the person you intended to be before the Crazy intervened and mutated your destiny.

These are all my hopes for you. I want to help you make bold and positive decisions. I want both you and your spouse to know peace. I imagine the two of you living a life of pure love.

My friend, I want you to know what it's like to simply enjoy a pleasant, serene day that easily blends into the next. And the next.

For many years now, I've pondered sharing my story. But I didn't feel ready to reveal such a dark phase of my life. Only if I could dredge up every nasty detail and expose my perceived failures as a husband would I be of any authentic service to the others out there in the same situation.

Well, that day has come, so watch your step—it's gonna get messy.

The time has arrived for me to pass these experiences on, even the pathetic ones. In doing so, my deepest wish is that you will soon travel your life-highway with less pain and despair because of one basic but monumental conclusion:

"I am not alone."

That's why this book.

◆ ◆ ◆

What Exactly is a Borderline Personality Disorder Anyway?

Is BPD all in a person's head? Is it like a virus? Is it contagious? Is it right in the middle of two other disorders?

These are all fair questions, and I have asked all of them at one time or another. When I first began to make inquiries, there were only a handful of books, and most of the internet articles I found were angry rants from spouses suggesting aggressive ways to keep a BP "in line." Yikes. Fortunately, the information available today is much better.

Let's look at what the personality-disorder experts say.

The "bible" used in the psychiatric profession to identify personality disorders is the *Diagnostic and Statistical Manual* (abbreviated as *DSM*). It is written by psychologists for other psychologists, so the language is rather clinical for the rest of us. It receives occasional updates, and the editions we will draw from are the fourth and fifth.

From the *DSM-IV*, BPD is a "pervasive pattern of instability of interpersonal relationships, self-image, and affects, and marked impulsivity beginning by early adulthood and present in a variety of contexts."

Like I said; the description is clinical. How about we give it a little real-world interpretation.

I would focus on the keywords "pervasive" and "variety." If the various symptoms listed between those two words aren't happening regularly *and* in lots of different places, we're not talking about BPD.

Makes sense, right? All of us have *some* BPD-like symptoms *some* of the time. Feeling occasionally unstable and impulsive hardly rates notice. But a Borderline presents these symptoms in an ongoing and extreme pattern.

Something else to keep in mind: expert clinical opinions are written to appear dispassionate and objective. They don't want to make it seem too personal.

I, on the other hand, am not bound by those limitations. So, when I read their perfunctory use of the word "pervasive," I know it really means "flailing, wailing, raging, jump-on-the-hood-of-a-moving-car-so-you-won't-leave-me."

In addition, "variety of contexts" means the Crazy will attack you anywhere it damn well wants, including: work, church, Walmart, school, the sidewalk, your parent's house, Saturday in the park, a hotel room, your best-friend's boat, Thanksgiving dinner, while you're sleeping, a birthday party, in the middle of sex, a movie theater, a restaurant, the doctor's office, or while sitting on a toilet.

What Causes BPD?

If a person has BPD, when did they get it and how long might it last? According to the Mayo Clinic, the disorder "usually begins by early adulthood" and "seems to be worse in young adulthood and may gradually get better with age."

Notice the qualifiers "usually," "seems," and "may" being used? This is a good example of how we really don't have definitive answers. There is a murky blend of chemical and environmental causes at work. So, no, it's not "all in their head." Sometimes a BP is a child of a BP parent. Other times, there are no signs of the disorder anywhere in the immediate family.

And no, BPD is not literally contagious or a virus. Although, it is common for the non-BP in a relationship to start acquiring BPD traits. After a while, all the wild behavior starts to feel normal enough that both people start acting that way.

I remember several times thinking, "Well, if she's going to accuse me of all these bad things, I might as well start doing some of them." Not exactly a healthy response on my part.

What's the Treatment?

Okay, after reading this book, you might conclude (if you haven't already) your wife is demonstrating BPD traits. Now you're wondering what the treatment is. There's a pill she can take, right? Nope. There are medications that seem to alleviate some of the symptoms (notice those wimpy qualifiers again), but there is no cure in a bottle.

Historically, BPD was considered very difficult to treat because the causes are hard to nail down. How do you correct something when you can't be sure where it originated and where it currently resides?

In recent years, there are more optimistic opinions about treatment. The Mayo Clinic says, "with newer, evidence-based treatment, many people with borderline personality disorder experience fewer and less severe symptoms, improved functioning, and an improved quality of life."

Notice they don't refer to a "cure" but instead use "fewer," "less severe," and "improved" to describe outcomes. That's better than nothing, but not overly optimistic.

There are, however, many people who self-report themselves as a "former" or "recovered" Borderline. That's a good sign. And there are many anecdotal accounts of those with BPD traits getting better with time. They eventually learn to work around the symptoms in a way that greatly reduces the impact on loved ones. That's also short of a cure, but at least there is space for healthy relationships to occur.

It appears, unfortunately, that the most hopeful treatment is found only in the passage of years, preferably under the guidance of extensive and ongoing therapy.

Two Categories of BPD

You won't find this in the "official" definitions, but among the BPD community it is common to break those with BPD into two categories: low and high functioning.

Those with low-functioning BPD are afflicted by a number of chronic debilitations that make them unable to function in normal society. This could come from overt physical abuse, drug overuse, alcoholism, and the presence of multiple mental disorders beyond BPD. This group is facing such severe problems that they are probably in constant treatment or institutionalization and not really what we're talking about in this book.

Our concern is the second group: high functioning. As you can guess, a high-functioning BP fits right in with day-to-day society. They are usually intelligent, creative, and successful in their career. Workmates and casual friends don't often witness any signs of BPD.

And if they do, the symptoms aren't pervasive and varied enough to look unusual. They are written off as normal stress and "having a bad day."

In a cruel twist, the full brunt of the BPD traits falls primarily on the inner circle of spouses, lovers, immediate family, and closest of friends. Those outside that circle often have no idea.

In fact, when I first began describing to select friends and family what I was experiencing due to my wife's BPD behavior, I had a hard time getting anyone to take me seriously. I'm sure they thought I was exaggerating or misinterpreting.

I would describe the wild rage-fests and they could only see the polite, sweet girl who made delicious homemade cookies. The Crazy is one crafty adversary to hide behind a tray of baked goodness.

◆ ◆ ◆

The Book Layout

The National Institute of Mental Health cites 12 symptoms of borderline personality disorder. The Mayo Clinic reduces the list to nine. The *DSM-5* from the American Psychiatric Association cites five main criteria with five sub-sets and 11 sub-sub-sets. The earlier *DSM-IV* cites nine symptoms (with at least five being required for a diagnosis).

There is enough correlation between these sources that I am confident introducing one primary symptom within each of 10 chapters, following loosely with the NIMH. Then I discuss a handful of remaining symptoms together in one of the final chapters.

The problem is, these "official" symptom descriptions are purposefully clinical and not always user friendly. Therefore, explanation and commentary are included from not only these sources but many others that express a more real-life character.

In other words, in each chapter, you'll receive an overview of what both the established experts and people-on-the-street are saying.

But this is the point where my book drastically deviates from any other you will find.

After the introductory portion of each chapter, I present multiple journal entries that I kept during the formative years of my BPD experience. Not simply quotes from others, but actual real-time accounts presented by me, the husband of a Borderline. As far as I have seen, **this is the first book written *by* a husband of BPD *for* husbands of BPD.**

As many of you might imagine, keeping a journal private from a BP is nearly impossible. The earliest entries were made in a computer document I had begun years before my marriage. But after noticing multiple revisions that were not made by me, I became suspicious.

Why would Lyssa have made edits to my journal? And why did the changes only involve comments about women from my past?

Confronting Lyssa only led to her denial and chastisement for not trusting her. Being new to marriage, I dismissed the underlying cause of her peculiar actions for the moment.

I wanted to keep journaling, but I apparently had to come up with a way of doing it that would remain authentic and private.

Ultimately, the solution was to use a laptop at work that I never removed from my office or connected to the internet. To avoid suspicion, I still occasionally made entries in the original document at home

Sneaky huh? It's amazing how much stupid shit we do when married to a BP, even before we know that's why we're doing it.

It was my dark secret, and I often felt like I was cheating on my wife by simply documenting what was occurring in those days. But, with the passing of time, those writings became a most precious possession.

These "in the moment" accounts are straight from the battlefield: unfiltered, full of confusion, ignorance, desperation, and perennial hope. I suspect you will often shout at the book, "HOLY CRAP! THAT'S EXACTLY WHAT HAPPENED TO ME!"

Yup. And to repeat my main theme: *you are not alone.*

Among these journal entries, I offer context based on subsequent years of self-reflection, academic study, and hours spent listening to Led Zeppelin recordings (I take answers wherever I find them). I believe these are the portions of the book that will offer the most unique learning potential and inspire you to take action in your life.

A warning: I am not a clinical psychologist or marriage counselor. I am not here to diagnose your spouse. In fact, many BPs never get officially diagnosed because they refuse to consider the possibility. But diagnosis is not the point.

It's not about hanging a label on your wife that says, "I told you it was all your fault!" At most, you'll likely just have to be content knowing your spouse has many of the traits associated with BPD. Giving the problem a name is incredibly helpful. That is enough for you to initiate a quest for improvements instead of assigning blame.

Keep in mind, you should not expect to drastically change the behavior of a Borderline. That's outside your control. But there is endless opportunity to change your interpretation of her actions and how you react to them. You can learn to set boundaries with clear consequences. While you can't make her change, you can certainly ask for changes in the way she treats you.

I am not an expert on *your* life. I am presenting what happened in *my* life and what I eventually did to save myself from destruction. It worked for me, amazingly so. A similar course might help you, or not. Choose your own path carefully.

Now, if you're ready to dig in and face the Crazy head on, keep reading.

CHAPTER 1: ABANDONMENT

BPDs may display efforts to avoid real or imagined abandonment, such as rapidly initiating intimate (physical or emotional) relationships or cutting off communication with someone in anticipation of being abandoned

The National Institute of Mental Health goes on to say:

> *Symptoms can be triggered by seemingly ordinary events; for example, people with borderline personality disorder may become angry and distressed over minor separations—due to business trips or changes in plans—from people to whom they feel close.*

Doesn't that quote sounds rather tame at first? "Angry and distressed" can have a wide range of meanings in a marriage.

You can imagine a fairly mild discussion between a married couple over coffee:

She says, "I was a bit upset at first when you talked about going to that trade show, but I understand it's an important part of your job that supports our family."

To which the husband replies, "Thanks babe. Your support means the world, and I'll be sure to reach out every night to tell you I miss you."

Awwww…so sweet. Now, let's run that same scenario through the filter of BPD:

Without any warning, she attacks with: "Don't you DARE think of going to that trade show. Why don't you EVER listen to my needs. I bet you're only going to meet that woman you used to work with. You're a HORRIBLE husband and I hope her plane crashes!"

To which the husband responds, "All I did was say there's a conference in Tulsa this year."

Fear of Abandonment

A key element for you to grasp about your wife is that as a BP, she has a greatly reduced or absent sense of self. If you're like me, that doesn't make much sense at first, so I'll walk you through it.

By your early adulthood, you developed a solid idea of who you are. Your core beliefs and morals were mostly baked in by this point. You had pieced together the various components that composed your self-identity. This allows you to now look in the mirror and say, "Hey good lookin;' we meet again."

That process never happened for your wife. For the moment, don't question how or why such a strange thing occurs. Just accept that it's your wife's truth.

Now, let yourself imagine how terrifying it must feel to be convinced you barely exist. From her perspective, she's only hanging onto life by the smallest threads of perception. The slightest shake or twist and *poof!* Nothingness.

In order for her to avoid facing the insanity of that situation, she assigns her existence to the person closer to her than anyone else: you! She transfers responsibility for her existence to her husband, and it becomes your job to provide the world shape and substance. You fill the nothingness that would surely obliterate her if not for your presence.

And yet, you have the absolutely horrific idea to spend some time with your friends this weekend instead of her? She wonders, how could you be such an insensitive fiend? Why can't you see the vacuum of empty space you are condemning her to? In her view, you and your friends are selfish cretins and the whole lot of you should die for your crimes!

Yup. And that's all before breakfast. It will get worse as the day progresses because you will handle it the same way I did—logically, rationally, based on a lifetime of experience—and completely wrong.

Merri Lisa Johnson, in *Girl in Need of a Tourniquet: Memoir of a Borderline Personality*, describes her need for love (and therefore, the opposite of abandonment) this way:

> I need to hear the words. "You win the prize. I will love you forever. You are worth losing everything else." Jackpot. Home base. An umpire whispers in my ear, "You're safe."

For you, it's a simple poker night with the guys. Or, at worst a work-related weekend out of town. For her, it's a potential death sentence. Without you providing the sense of self she doesn't have,

25

she goes "poof" and evaporates into the ether. She demands that you love her enough to keep that from happening.

I'm not expecting you to believe her fear of abandonment makes logical sense, but I'm telling you to grasp that *she* believes it's true with all her heart. In the heat of the moment, her brain is 100% convinced that your absence will doom her to oblivion.

Here are some samples from my journal regarding fear of abandonment. Maybe you've faced similar events.

Abandonment Example #1

Year 1, January:

We got back from an awesome honeymoon today. Three days in the mountains. I was tired after the drive home and unpacking so went to take a nap. Lyssa and I ended up having our first married argument because she didn't like me leaving her alone. She asked something about "What am I supposed to do while you're sleeping?" "Whatever you want" I said. Weird.

To me, it was just a nap like anyone might take. To her, she was seeing her new husband choose to do something without her for the first time.

The BP mind begins twisting a new narrative: "If he can just walk off to another room without me, he must not love me as much as I thought. I bet it's all a big joke to him. He's going to leave me; I just know it. I can't let him do this!"

She wasn't trying to stop me from taking a nap. She was trying to stop me from abandoning her to a world of nothingness. Big difference. Of course, I had no clue and only found her attitude odd and annoying.

It's hard to find common ground when I'm looking at a cat nap and she's seeing the end of existence.

Another entry from later that month reads:

Today she said, "Wouldn't it be great if we spend our entire marriage without a single night apart?" I said that sounds pretty unrealistic with the careers both of us are pursuing that often involve travel. She got very upset that I wouldn't somehow figure out a way to never be away from her. What was I supposed to do; lie that I thought it was a reasonable expectation?

In a word, yes. She wanted me to lie, but she wouldn't have heard it that way. The lie from my mouth would have fallen on her ears as armor against the fear of being alone.

She was able to control most of her BPD traits in the beginning of our marriage, but her abandonment issues showed up again only a few months later.

Year 1, April:
We had another argument. She seems so ready to find problems. It's gotten to where I just leave the apartment to let her cool off. Today she asked me to promise I'll never leave until an argument is resolved. That sounds overly idealistic but she seemed so desperate for me to agree. Whatever.

Jump ahead another few months to see how quickly things escalated:

Year 1, June:

She totally lost it today and started throwing shit around the living room. I couldn't take it so I grabbed my car keys and left. She followed me to the parking lot screaming the whole way that I promised not to leave during an argument. I was betraying her and a coward. Neighbors were watching.

I started my truck and pulled out when she jumped on the hood! I kept driving for a while because I just couldn't fathom what was happening. She was on the hood of a fucking moving car to keep me from leaving! This is crazy stuff you see in a movie.

I parked in a different spot, got out and started walking down the street. She followed, crying and pleading for me to wait. I began running to get away. My only thought was to get away from this crazy person. She screamed and collapsed. The crazy person was my wife who was suffering. I went back to her.

To make that particular situation all the more surreal, what did I get for returning to her? She insisted that I owed her an apology. She took no responsibility for her choices. I made her jump on my hood. Yup.

In my ignorance, I was reacting as if she was capable of a rational response. I wanted to leave in order to defuse a volatile situation. My leaving triggered the feelings that her universe was imploding on itself.

She was damaged. But she didn't want to admit it, so she instead turned those feelings on me. *I* was the screwed up one. *I* was the crazy dude running down a street rather than confronting a sweet, cookie-baking girl.

And yet, she also viewed me as the only thread connecting her to existence. The above journal entry depicts a truly awful day for me. But hers was a thousand times worse. While I ran away to find calm, her demons gathered over her for the feast.

What I Wish I Had Done:

With what I know now, what might I have done differently that day? When the argument was beginning to get out of control, I wish I had said:

> "I can tell you're very upset about this. I get that. But this level of intensity is making me feel like I need to leave. I know you don't think leaving is a good solution, but I'm entitled to feel differently and might need to do it to feel safe. Maybe you'll feel worse if that happens but that's your choice. Let's just take 30 minutes of being quiet and try to talk again later."

Notice how I'm trying to empathize with her fear of abandonment while not accusing her of anything? Furthermore, I'm taking responsibility for my own feelings, but not any misbehaviors she had accused me of. Then, I suggest an outcome and how it is tied into choices we make.

Would that have worked? Maybe not. But it would have kept her off the hood and me from running down the sidewalk like a lunatic.

By the way, a day later a co-worker said, "Dude, I was driving down the street and saw you jogging along with your wife way behind you. Did you have car trouble or something?" Yeah, it was car trouble all right.

The ultimate example of her struggle with abandonment displayed itself the day she had me arrested and ultimately prosecuted for felony abuse.

Year 3, April:
I can't believe this! I spent the night in jail because of her! All because I tried to leave the house in the middle of a disagreement. I tried desperately to get her out of the way. I finally pushed her and she got the smallest cut on her finger. That's all it took. She fucking had me arrested. We are done!

We weren't done.

I ended up meeting with a divorce attorney and he explained how I would look like the bad guy. A judge would award her everything she wanted, including public sympathy. I would forever be the abusive asshole with a criminal record. The judicial system is simply not designed to protect spouses of a BP. The Borderline looks like a believable victim. I don't.

When I told her I was divorcing her, she completely freaked out. Apparently, I was supposed to apologize and tell her how much I appreciated her love for me. When I went the opposite way, she was shocked and began to panic.

She tried to drop the charges, but the judicial system didn't allow for that. Too many abused women are bullied into changing their story, so courts take over the role of plaintiff. That way the woman is no longer the one making the charge.

This makes perfect sense for conventional cases of domestic abuse. But when the spouse is on the wrong end of a Borderline's false or exaggerated accusations, he's screwed.

I was horribly conflicted by my own actions surrounding this event. I *had* pushed her out of the way. Should that result in a felony domestic violence conviction? And what about the fact that she refused to let me leave? Isn't that a form of kidnapping? But, but...I'm the man and it's always wrong to lay hands on a woman, right?

I had never been in any situation like that before. Heck, I had spent my adult life considering myself a peaceful, sensitive guy who could always talk his way through a disagreement. Now, core aspects of my self-image were being challenged. How did I get in this mess and how would I get out of it?

I ended up pleading guilty. That was one of the worst days of my life. Until the next one. And the next.

Still, I didn't leave my wife. She pleaded with me that things would now be better. I kept reminding myself that real men don't give up on a marriage. We fight to solve the problems. We protect our women. We fix things that are broken. We turn our lowest day into the rallying cry for our greatest accomplishment!

We also apply bullshit male bravado to situations that require a completely different response. I was such a boob.

◆ ◆ ◆

Couples who have been married a while can relate to the concept that not all arguments are about what they are arguing about.

She might be complaining at you for not taking out the trash, but what she's really mad about is that thing you did a week ago you have no memory of. A healthy couple can even find the humor in these moments.

When married to a BP, this disconnect happens at an EXTREME level and there's nothing funny about it. **It's a safe assumption that most all of the seemingly random outbursts made by a BP can be traced to fears of abandonment.** This was definitely true in my early years with Lyssa.

Her constant false accusations regarding my behavior around other women (or even representations of women) were the most common example. And even *that* issue would become couched in other arguments, to the point where abandonment was a few generations removed. But it was always the prime motivator, although I didn't know it until much later.

And silly me. I would spend my time responding to, and defending myself against, the literal accusation being made, which of course was wasted effort. While I bashed my head against a brick wall confronting the thing she was actually talking about, Lyssa would get increasingly upset because the root problem never got addressed.

The process would go like this:

--She would express upset over thing 1
--I would respond (defensively) to thing 1
--She would get more upset because I was not getting the point (that had nothing to do with thing 1)
--I would respond with even more vigor to thing 1
--She would abandon thing 1 and accuse me of thing 2

--I would get spun around and begin defending myself against thing 2. Sometimes I would insist that we stick to thing 1.
--Either way, she would now insist on an apology for the horrible way I was treating her, which would now become thing 3 to argue over
--I would spend a couple days furious that she seemed to seek out confrontation over pathetically unimportant issues
--She would recover much sooner and wonder why I was still upset
--Days later, she'd bring up thing 1 again and the cycle would start over

Sound familiar to your life? When you argue with a BP, no matter how many issues you think you've "explained" away, the list of transgressions will never get shorter. The moment you feel an item has been crossed off the top, she's added three more to the bottom.

And the horrible insanity of all the lost hours and days spent arguing is that it turns out nothing on the "list" actually mattered. It was all just a redirection of the real problem. But we'll fight to our last breath over thing 1, forever convinced that our BP wife is actually mad about the thing she says she's mad about.

Abandonment Example #2

In our first month of dating, we went to a mall on a warm summer day, and I commented on some young ladies all wearing skimpy t-shirts to the point it seemed to be a required uniform for their age group.

Lyssa immediately became upset and said she didn't appreciate me looking at other women when we were together. Her reaction didn't seem without merit. I didn't think I had been leering, but

ROBERT PAGE

maybe I could be more thoughtful. It actually tugged at my old-school chivalry. I apologized and thought that was the end of it.

Hardly. That issue became the mutating germ that simply would not die. As it took on numerous and evolved forms, I never knew it was only ever about a single issue—abandonment.

Year 1, May:

I gave Lyssa a lovely Hallmark birthday card today. I added several sweet sentences of my own. He first response after reading it was, "Where did you get this card?" I told her, "From the mall." She became very agitated and questioned why I would go there. "Because that's where the Hallmark store is and they have the nicest cards," I answered. I gave her a nice card and all it did was make her mad. What's wrong with this picture?

She wasn't responding to the card at all. The Crazy was telling her, "He just goes there to look at half-dressed girls because he doesn't really love you."

Here's another entry from that same time period:

My mom gave Lyssa a Victoria's Secret gift card and I said something like, "Ooh baby, are you gonna pick out some sexy items like those models in the pictures?" She completely freaked out and accused me of wanting to have sex with poster-girls. My mom was being thoughtful about sending a gift to her new daughter-in-law, and Lyssa turns it into some sort of perversion on my part.

Again, it wasn't about the thing she was expressing upset about (sexy models). Her BP mind was saying, "He wants to have sex with those women because I'm not good enough. He'll figure out there's something wrong with me and leave. I'll attack him first and tell him how awful he is so he'll feel guilty and stay."

But because she couldn't articulate the core problem of abandonment, Lyssa simply condemned me for a convenient problem of her own invention. Victoria's Secret and the mall where the store was located became a regular target of her stress.

She insisted that I refrain from going to the mall without her. And if I had to go, she wanted me to avoid walking by any "adult" store. If we went there together, she would make sure we crossed the walkway to the opposite side of the offending storefronts.

As an extended response, she also asked me to promise to always look away when a Victoria's Secret commercial appeared on television, even if she wasn't there.

As you can imagine, I found all these requests (demands, really) preposterous. For the rest of my life, I'm supposed to look away from various TV commercials? How could I honestly agree to that?

We spent hours of our life arguing about the completely absurd topic of Victoria's Secret. Of course, the reality was that while I argued with passionate logic about thing 1, it was never about that.

But wait, there's more...

The "you want to have sex with everyone" accusations only escalated with time. It got to the point that I avoided going shopping nearly anywhere with Lyssa because of her strange behaviors.

At the supermarket, Lyssa developed the habit of getting very affectionate while we waited in line to check out. At first it was clinging to me. Then asking me to look her in the eyes and kiss her. Finally, she was throwing herself into full open-mouth making out. I'm no prude, and a little PDA is fine, but this was the kind of thing that would make me think, "Get a room," if I saw others doing it.

When I confronted her and explained how I didn't feel comfortable with her actions, she accused me of being thoughtless. "I'm just letting you know how attracted I am to you and you can't handle it."

It seemed so weird. Why was this happening in a checkout line and nowhere else? Something was obviously triggering her BPD, but I have to admit it was years before I figured it out.

It was the magazines in the rack.

She never admitted it, but I'm sure they were the source of her discomfort. Like most shoppers (at least the store managers would hope), I let my eyes fall across the magazine covers while waiting in line. In Lyssa's view, I was seeing only the sexy models and unable to control urges to have sex with them, ultimately leading to my abandoning her.

Her response to this dilemma? Crank up her own sexuality so that I wouldn't have a need to see anyone but her. My discomfort with her behavior only confirmed her viewpoint that I didn't find her sexy and wasn't really in love.

In a rare glimpse into the deep origins of her BPD traits, she mentioned that when she was young, her mother would often flip the magazines backwards in the checkout lane as she waited with her children.

Lyssa's mom performed that action in a helicopter-parent attempt to protect her kids from unsavory adult content. Her daughter carried that same behavior into her marriage but with a different, far unhealthier motive.

The same type of problem occurred during our trips to Walmart.

Year 1, June:

Today at Walmart Lyssa got furious at me over such a simple thing. When approaching the checkout stand, I noticed a rack with CDs and saw that a young female pop star had a greatest hits disc. I picked it up and couldn't help chuckle at the fact that an artist that young already had enough hits to warrant a best-of release. Lyssa scolded me to put the CD down and stop making a fool of myself drooling over the picture. Whether the singer looked hot was not even on my mind. I hate the way she treats me like a total perv.

This was not the only time Walmart was a problem. She once chastised me in the middle of a crowded aisle, "Why do you always make sure we walk through the girls' underwear section?"

Another time she scolded me for staring at the posters of hair-style models outside the salon. "Why do you always have to stare at those women?" I had no idea what she was talking about. In my mind I'm just walking through a store with stuff around me that may or may not fall in my field of vision.

As you can imagine, I would become defensive to these bizarre accusations and we would quickly cascade into arguments lasting hours. The entire time I'm getting angrier that she keeps wasting so much of our marriage picking fights about things that didn't even happen.

In exasperation, I remember once shouting at her, "Just once I wish you'd start a fight over something we both think is a real thing." That didn't go over well.

For Lyssa, every argument was life-and-death real. The struggle was constant in her mind. If I considered anyone else sexy, I must therefore want to have sex with them, which could only lead to one outcome: abandonment and her utter non-existence.

What I Wish I Had Done:

My solution at the time of these events was to simply limit exposure to the places that caused her stress. One by one, I eliminated the mall, supermarket, or department stores from places we could go together. Rather than try to understand the problem and perhaps resolve it, I just cut those locations out of daily activity.

This course of action certainly reduced our arguments about malls and stores, but the number of arguments never decreased. Her list of perceived transgressions was inexhaustible and she would quickly transfer her fear of abandonment to other subjects and locations.

The better solution would have been to set clear boundaries and consequences. Before leaving our home, I wish I would have said:

"I understand that you don't like the idea of a husband staring at pictures of women on walls and magazines. I'm sure that's very upsetting when you think it's happening. But I'm equally as convinced that I don't do those things in any sort of disrespectful way, and I get frustrated feeling falsely accused. I want to have fun shopping with you today, but know that if I feel we're entering into an argument, I will leave and find my own ride home. You can choose to have a fun time or you can choose to make accusations that upset both of us. It's up to you."

Coming up with a statement like the above takes considerable thought. And delivering such boundaries will not be easy. It might even cause an argument of its own. To top it off, setting boundaries may not always work.

A BP will constantly challenge and make countermoves to anything you try. They don't easily accept the suggestion that their feelings aren't more important than yours. Insisting that your opinion deserves just as much consideration won't go over well.

But it's not about making abrupt changes in a day. The plan is to set boundaries and consequences that over weeks and months become more normalized.

You're striving for small changes over the long term. And just a reminder, most of these changes will be coming from *you*, not your wife.

Now, on to the next "extreme" symptom.

CHAPTER 2: EXTREMES

*BPDs tend to view things in extremes, such as all
good or all bad, and their opinions of other people
can also change quickly, leading to intense and
unstable relationships*

This chapter is centered on the *roses and rage* theme I use in my BPD book titles. And for good reason—it's all about extremes. One moment you're enjoying lovely, quality time with your wife. And within a flash the two of you are in a verbal knife fight spiraling out of control.

Such extremes are an all-too-common trait of BPD and a major cause for difficulty in a marriage. Billy Joel explains it nicely in his song "I Go to Extremes:"

> *Too high or too low, there ain't no in betweens*
> *And if I stand or I fall, it's all or nothing at all*
> *Darling, I don't know why I go to extremes*

A BP tends to view people in their inner circle as all good or bad. The same person can be reassigned the opposite designation within a dramatically short period of time. You can be considered one or the other, but not a combination of both in the same instant. To a non-BP, this is a wild roller coaster of emotions.

For another context, the *DSM-5* states that the close relationships of a BP are "often viewed in extremes of idealization and devaluation and alternating between over involvement and withdrawal."

Let's unpack some of that language.

One day your BP wife considers you the ideal husband. She is cheerful and appreciative. You can do no wrong and have completely transformed her life for the better. This is her *idealization* of you.

Then, with what feels like no warning, she rages how you can't be trusted, are worthless around the house, don't make enough money to support the family, and if she has an affair it will be your fault. This is her *devaluation* of you.

These extreme viewpoints might also correspond to equally extreme involvement (she won't let you out of her sight) and withdrawal (she disappears for a weekend and won't tell you where she's been).

You're left spinning in a blur of ups and downs, not sure which extreme you should believe, or perhaps neither.

Splitting
The act of a BP swinging wildly between idolizing and demonizing a person is also called "splitting." In *Stop Walking on Eggshells: Taking Your Life Back When Someone You Care About Has Borderline Personality*

Disorder, authors Paul Mason and Randi Kreger describe splitting this way:

> *Because people with BPD have a hard time integrating a person's good and bad traits, their current opinion of someone is often based on their last interaction with them.*

While most people have the ability to cope with contradictions and grey areas, a BP sees only good or evil and has no memory of previously assigning one label to a person while in the clutch of the polar opposite. The BP exists in an all-or-nothing world.

As the husband of a BP, you are both her savior and destroyer. But not at the same time. Unlike you, she has no quandary shifting between those extremes.

While you develop an opinion about a person that might last a lifetime, she requires little convincing to completely dismiss one impression for another. And those on the receiving end of this whiplash are left dazed and confused.

The BP's all-or-nothing worldview also applies to how they view themselves through you. Offering only the slightest criticism may result in a harsh reaction. This is because the BP can't conceive of a partial dislike.

You might tell your wife that you couldn't read one of the words in a letter she wrote and her response is, "I'm not stupid. I don't know why you're always calling me such an idiot! Why did you even marry me in the first place?" I would respond to Lyssa at times like this with comments like, "Whoa! Sounds like you've skipped over a few possibilities and gone straight to red alert."

For me, it was these kinds of out-of-the-blue attacks that began chipping away at my previously talkative personality. After experiencing enough splitting, I spoke to Lyssa much less. When I couldn't predict what kinds of topics might trigger the Crazy, it became safer to just keep my mouth shut.

Here is a relevant journal entry.

Year 3, February:

Last night we were watching the Simpsons one minute and had one of the biggest fights of our marriage the next. There was a scene where Marge gets caught outside in only a bath towel that is accidentally dropped. I chuckled lightly. That was all it took. BAM! "How could you think that's funny? What kind of sick person are you? I don't know why you think it's okay to laugh at porn on our TV! I don't ever want you watching that show again!"

The Simpsons? Porn?

"Apologize for laughing at that scene," she kept insisting. "I can't be married to someone who thinks that's funny. Take it back!"

What is wrong with her? We were up all night. She wouldn't let me sleep because I wouldn't apologize for thinking the Simpsons is a funny show.

Obviously, the *Simpsons* does not represent porn. But the Crazy was in complete charge the moment I chuckled at the idea of Marge being caught outside in the nude.

What happened? She split me. Her BP mind was not able to consider that a naked body in a TV show was not porn, even if that cartoon body was not shown onscreen or in a sexual nature. Porn is porn.

Furthermore, if her husband sees a porn object, he *must* want to have sex with it, which means he will find someone else more attractive than her and leave. This will happen because he is a vile, disgusting creature capable of only horrid actions. Her solution to this lightning-fast conclusion was to attack me first before I committed the crime she imagined me plotting.

All that because I chuckled at the *Simpsons* and refused to "take it back." Can a chuckle even be taken back?

Here's an example of a similar event that occurred earlier:

Year 2, June:
Lyssa has always loved the movie The Shining, *which I hadn't seen, so she rented a copy for us to watch. Before it began, she said, "There's a scene I want you to promise you won't watch. I'll tell you when you can open your eyes." I asked if she would be closing her eyes as well and she said, "No!" like it was a stupid question.*

The scene she was concerned about showed a woman getting out of a bathtub. It is meant to be scary and disturbing, not sexual. But, as before, Lyssa only saw porn and her husband packing his bags to find that actress and have sex with her.

I'm a big Pink Floyd fan. So, when the drummer published a memoir, I brought it home from the library and began reading it in bed that night. Lyssa saw what was in my hands and gasped.

It hadn't even registered with me that the back cover features a photograph of four women whose naked backs are painted to feature artwork from iconic Pink Floyd album covers. The women are seated, facing away from the camera, and only if you look hard you can make out a touch of butt crack.

Lyssa flipped out about me bringing smut into our house and that I was some sort of pervert for wanting to read that book. I tried to explain why none of that made sense, but logic has no meaning to an upset BP. I refused to not read the book, so her solution was to attach paper over the back cover to obscure the image.

These examples of "porn is porn" were a mess at the time, but come off as a bit humorous when I look back at them. Another instance, however, was just plain sad because it meant Lyssa and I would likely not be able to view many great movies from that point on.

Lyssa had never seen *Schindler's List* so I brought home a copy. I was excited to be able to share this powerful story and one of my favorite movies. Lyssa being a classical music fan, I especially thought she'd appreciate the soundtrack featuring Itzhak Pearlman. We never got that far.

Earlier in the film is a devasting scene where women are made to run in circles without clothes while the German officials rank their health for processing. It is the antithesis of sexual. Didn't matter. Porn is porn.

Lyssa was horrified I had "set her up" to watch such a disgusting scene "full of naked women." We weren't able to finish the movie because she wouldn't tolerate "smut." As usual, she wanted me to apologize for my horrid behavior.

Apologize for *Schindler's List* being smutty? Yup. The same scenario played out when we tried to watch the *Godfather* together. Can you think of any smutty scenes in that movie? Neither could I. She found one. This is what life is like married to a BP.

One other example of splitting involved how she thought I might perceive *her* as "all bad."

Year 2: November
Today I was stunned to find Lyssa in the back yard smoking a cigarette. I asked when she started smoking and she said, "I've always stress smoked, but I never told you because you said when we started dating you wouldn't date a woman who smokes." She's right, I wouldn't.

Lyssa had deceived me for about two years because had I learned she was a smoker, even after we were married, she was convinced I would reach an all-or-nothing judgement and immediately leave her.

This was an amazing deception on her part. On the contrary, I did not leave her for smoking. In fact, we found ways to incorporate it into our household so that she could continue to use smoking as a stress relief. I didn't like it, but I was willing to make the after-the-fact concession.

However, it is certainly true that I would not have continued dating her after learning she sometimes smoked. My apologies to you smokers out there, but that's my preference. By hiding such a detail, she stripped me of my choice in the matter. In a sense, her extreme BPD anxieties were correct on this particular issue.

By the time some of these events were occurring, I had become aware of BPD, but I still hadn't directly connected it to what was going on. I vaguely understood there was a correlation, but I mostly held on to the idea that it was just Lyssa being weird about "adult content," especially in light of her childhood.

Brought up in a sequestered home where there was little interaction with people outside of family and church, Lyssa was raised to be suspicious of media in all its forms. There were hundreds of books and videos available in the home, but they were all meticulously prescreened by her parents.

When visiting, I perused the enormous book collection and noticed several instances of homemade redactions with black ink. In addition, most of the videos had come from a service that removed sensitive content, downgrading all of them to a rated G level. Censorship was standard behavior in that home.

Rather than completely assign our marriage problems to BPD as I should have, I instead began making connections to her upbringing. I would tell myself, "She's just overreacting to the restrictions she grew up with. Give her some time and she'll grow out of it. I'll just have to try harder to be understanding."

Over and over again, I would take the responsibility for Lyssa's actions. That's what strong men do, right? They shelter their wives from the big scary world. Eventually, the wives feel safe and *everything* is okay. I kept waiting...and waiting.

How Did I First Learn of BPD?

It wasn't until well into our second year of marriage that I first heard the words "borderline personality disorder." I remember thinking it was a lousy term and wondering, "Is that just the placeholder name until they come up with the real one?"

(As it turns out, there was considerable discussion during the writing of the *DSM-5* to do away with the name "borderline personality disorder" and choose another, but it didn't happen.)

As I mentioned in the introduction, Lyssa had us promise to each other soon after our wedding that we would not discuss marriage problems with friends or family. Having never been married before, this sounded reasonable to me, and I couldn't think of a reason to disagree at the time.

I truly believe she also had not heard of BPD before our marriage. But she did occasionally mention having panic attacks and that she desperately needed me to help calm her when they happened.

So, while she didn't suspect BPD, she definitely knew she had emotional or mental problems. And her subconscious (the Crazy) was already taking steps to hide the problems from me by assuring I didn't discuss anything with others.

If I never compared notes with my married friends, I wouldn't have clarity that anything was unusual. I would comfort myself by thinking, "I bet all new marriages have the same problems we're facing."

The majority of our most horrid arguments fell into this period of my ignorance. Her raging was a stunning demonstration of emotional violence.

Threats of suicide, physically attacking me, "splitting" me into an angel and devil, desperate attempts to keep me from leaving during an argument, putting both of us in danger, attempts to erase my past so that I would depend on her for my identity, assuming my identity in emails to my work associates and former girlfriends; all these BPD traits were in full force during the first year or two of marriage. But I didn't know they had a name.

...until one day...

In the second year of marriage with Lyssa, I had reached a pivotal moment. The fights and threats had risen beyond the pale. But I still hoped that our situation fell within the normal range on the "average marriage" scale. With these mixed feelings, I decided to break my vow of silence and reach out to others for context.

Reviewing my list of close friends and family, I purposely omitted most from potential contact because if I was wrong about my growing concerns for Lyssa's mental health, I didn't want to poison the opinions of too many people. Ever the protective husband.

First, I selected a married couple who had known both of us during our early dating months. Second, I chose to call two brothers who had many years of experience being married. Last, I included a married best friend who had known me for 20 years, met Lyssa during a shared vacation weekend, and would give it to me straight.

Both the best friend and my brothers listened patiently to my accounts of recent arguments and bizarre behavior. When I concluded, I asked sincerely, "So, do you have this kind of stuff happen too and it's just an unspoken secret that all husbands keep?" The answer was a resounding "NO!"

They half wondered if I was joking and couldn't grasp that I was actually not sure if Lyssa's behavior was normal. One by one they pronounced I was in a messed-up relationship in need of immediate intervention.

In my defense, and defense of all BP husbands out there, the Crazy sneaks up on you, real quiet like. One strange thing happens, and you think, "Okay, that's odd, but I guess I can handle it. After all, she's my wife and I love her." Then another strange thing. And another. Soon, the horrific becomes normalized.

It's like the parable of the frog who never jumps out of the pot of water as it slowly begins to boil. By the time you notice the heat, you're cooked.

So, there it was. Validation from three trusted mates that I was *not* in a normal relationship. Check. But that opens up a pile of problems as well. Now I have to figure out what *is* wrong, *why* it's happening, and *what* I can do about it. That's where Dan and Sandra came in.

They were the married couple who knew Lyssa during my doctorate program and we had all spent more than a few nights together at the local Mexican cantina. After first speaking with Dan, he said, "We need Sandra on this." She was a social worker with years of experience around troubled households.

After repeating most of what I just said to Dan, Sandra asked the question that forever changed my outlook on Lyssa and our relationship:

"Have you ever heard of borderline personality disorder?"

Like many other key moments in a person's life, such as when a child is born, where you were when 9/11 happened, or having sex for the first time, I think all spouses of borderline personality disorder can recall the first time they heard those three words.

Sandra went on to describe her mother's BPD and how what I was describing seemed eerily similar. She walked me through the basics and shared what she went through growing up. Ultimately, she didn't like what she was hearing and sounded pessimistic about our future.

She closed the conversation by saying, "You know Rob, life's too short to waste a minute of it suffering voluntarily. You can choose not to. It's up to you." Dire words.

I thanked her for the insight, but internally dismissed her warning. Even if Lyssa did have this BPD stuff, I'm sure I could find a way to make it better. After all, she was my wife, and that's what a good husband is supposed to do; be a rock against any storm. Right?

Projecting and Therapist #1

Because a BP views the world as good and bad and they don't want to view themselves as bad, they often "project" any negative qualities onto the people around them, especially a spouse.

During our first years of marriage, Lyssa berated me, physically attacked me, threatened suicide if I didn't agree to her demands, destroyed personal property, stole and hid items she knew I cared about, and insisted I cease contact with several female friends.

Yet, one day she sternly announced that she would no longer tolerate my verbal abuse and wanted me to read a book that described my wrongdoings.

Do you recall my account of being put in jail even though it was my wife who started off the day by imprisoning me in my own home? That night she told the judge she wanted my punishment to include anger management because I had a nasty temper (he obliged).

After speaking with the judge, she didn't want to stay alone at the house, but rather than contact a friend, she called for a bed at the battered women's shelter. *I* was the one on the receiving end of her rage, yet *she* was the abused spouse.

These are all painfully real examples of projection. Consider for a moment how you would defend yourself against accusations that not only offend your core principles, but are being done *to* you rather than *by* you. This is what you will likely face if you stay married to a BP long enough.

Oddly enough, it was Lyssa's projecting that brought the words "borderline personality disorder" to our doorstep. She was convinced that if only *I* was more sensitive and less prone to angry outbursts, we could have a better relationship. As flip-flopped as that was, her solution was that we begin marriage counseling. I jumped at the chance.

The sessions started off simply enough. The psychologist, Dr. Thornton, walked us through basic communication techniques with an emphasis on listening without judgement. We tried to use them in our daily lives but seemed more interested in weaponizing the tools to prove our own viewpoints.

The truth was, neither of us was in counseling for the right reasons. I was there mostly to prove to anyone outside my marriage that I wasn't nuts, and my wife was there to prove that I was the abusive one in the relationship.

After a few sessions, it was clear that Dr. Thornton was no longer focusing on me. Nearly the entire hour was spent talking with Lyssa. She noticed it too, and after a couple weeks she confronted him: "Why aren't you asking Rob about *his* problems?" After all, it was her husband who needed the help, not her.

Then it happened...a most surreal moment. Dr. Thornton said, "I'd like the two of you to read this information I have on borderline personality disorder and let me know what you think."

BOOM! It was like Lyssa had just been blasted through a wall! And boy was she pissed. "Who do you think you are? How dare you? You don't know anything about me!" The man calmly replied, "I'm just a country doctor at heart. If it walks like a duck and quacks like a duck, I'm thinking it might be a duck."

On the drive home, Lyssa announced I was not allowed to give credence to anything we had just heard. I stayed quiet as I made sure the BPD pamphlet stayed hidden in my pocket.

Yeah, we never went back to Doctor Duck again.

Moving on, let's talk about mood swings.

CHAPTER 3: MOOD SWINGS

BPDs may display intense and highly changeable
moods, with each episode lasting from a few hours
to a few days, along with uncertainty about how
they see themselves and their role in the world

As you can see, the symptom of mood swings is related to the extreme views discussed in the last chapter. The difference is that this symptom deals specifically with how the BP is acting, rather than their viewpoint about another person.

The *DSM-5* refers to an "emotional liability" demonstrated by the following:

> *Unstable emotional experiences and frequent mood changes; emotions*
> *that are easily aroused, intense, and/or out of proportion to events and*
> *circumstances.*

Interestingly, the *DSM-5* did away with the time reference of "a few hours to a few days" as found in the *DSM-IV* and other literature. I assume this means the authors are more concerned about the mood swings being present at all, rather than how long they last.

Going along with general descriptions for a moment, there is a difference between the mood swings of a BP and someone acting bipolar. The BP will usually shift between moods at a much faster rate. And once they arrive at the new mood, they have little awareness of the one recently vacated. It's all or nothing.

The authors of the excellent *Stop Walking on Eggshells* describe how the mood of a BP "may swing from intense anger to depression, depression to irritability, and irritability to anxiety within a few hours." They add, "Non-BPs often find this unpredictability exhausting."

Exhausting is right. There were several nights Lyssa subjected me to sleep deprivation by ripping the bedding and sheets away from me, turning on all the lights in the house, yanking pillows from under my head, and insisting that I engage her in an argument.

There I would be, naked on a bare mattress in the middle of night, the house fully lighted, knowing I have to leave for work in a few hours, and her in the grips of yet another mood swing. No amount of logical discussion or rational pleading had any affect.

Usually, the outcome would be that after hours of my refusing to engage at her level of intensity, I would finally snap due to lack of sleep and meet her rage with an equal force. It was not pretty. At various times I broke a lamp, put a hole in a door, and knocked around the furniture—all actions I had never before committed.

The end results? I would be furious for days, while her mood would quickly swing back to pleasant. It was as if my eventual intense response allowed her to relax. The next day, she would criticize me for still being angry and insist on an apology. Yup. I owed *her* an apology.

I tell you, BPD sucks.

Sometimes her mood swings would occur in public or dangerous locations as related in this journal entry that refers to Janice, the last woman I dated before Lyssa.

Year 2, Sep:

We spent last week driving cross country on the interstate. We were having a great time and chatting casually about the sites. Then we had a few silent moments, and that's all it took. She brought up the usual: "Promise me you'll never contact Janice ever again or even think about her." As always, I insisted that is impossible for a human to agree to. "Sometimes a brain randomly thinks of people you used to know. It happens."

She pulled over to the narrow emergency lane and refused to move the car for about a half hour. This was a precarious spot and I actually considered our lives in danger. I finally got her to agree to exit at the next offramp. We parked in front of a corporate office. She got out and refused to drive any further or give me the keys until I agreed to her concessions. She also grabbed the sunglasses from my face in the bright sun so that I would be uncomfortable and more likely to fold.

A security guard pulled up and said we would have to leave their private lot. I said, "I'd love to. Talk to her." He said he was calling a tow truck. I finally convinced her that if she didn't get in the car I would simply walk off, find an airport, fly home, and file for divorce. It worked.

That night at a hotel she couldn't understand why I was still so livid. She was completely calm and asked if we could make love. I felt like throwing up.

Her taking the keys, stranding us somewhere, and refusing to get in the car was a common tactic in her war against common sense. It's a helpless feeling when someone in an adult body erupts in a tantrum like a 3-year-old.

In a dangerous or unacceptable situation with a child, you can simply pick them up and move. But do that to a woman and they arrest you for assault. So, you stand there, helpless, trying make deals with security guards. Or you lose patience and do something stupid.

I tried everything I could think of, multiple times. None of it worked. The Crazy won every time.

Once, we were driving on a Kentucky backroad while camping at a state park. It was a beautiful area and we'd been enjoying ourselves. Then, her dark side took over and she accused me of gawking inappropriately at some women walking along the road.

With all we had been through before, I knew the only possible outcome was her rage and ruin. So, I pre-emptively turned ugly and said, "Just knock it off right now. You know you're just trying to start a fight for absolutely no reason." What was her response? She jumped out of the car WHILE WE WERE MOVING!

Fortunately, I was driving quite slow leaving an intersection. I stopped and yelled for her to "get back in the car or I'm leaving you wherever the hell we are." She refused. I drove away.

That's right people! *I left my wife on the side of a highway in Kentucky.* That's how messed up I was. Disgusting behavior like that had actually become a reasonable reaction.

As I drove off, I noted in the mirror that she was walking the same direction. After several miles, the gravity of my choice sank in and I told myself, "Hey asshole, maybe you should make sure your wife doesn't end up in a bunker somewhere being told 'It puts the lotion on its skin.'"

When I found her, she again refused to get in the car. I drove along the side of the road for another mile or so before she finally got tired and yielded.

She had been falsely accusing me of bad behavior for a couple years by this time, and to my horror, I was acquiring the very behaviors I was convinced were hers alone. Her lightning fast mood swings were infecting me with an equal response. We were both becoming very unstable people.

So, was that the last straw? Did she finally see the writing on the wall that the issue of BPD might be something to consider? Nope.

But she did find a new couple's therapist for us so she could continue her efforts to fix *me*.

Therapist #2

I had admitted to Lyssa that I was talking to friends about our problems, so she began doing the same, although I'm sure I was the bad guy in those discussions. But in a strange way, taking the fall for her felt like an honorable act. It was one of the few things I could do that felt like a contribution.

One of her friends suggested a clerical marriage counselor who had helped her parents. Lyssa and I weren't religious, but if she was willing to try counseling again, I wasn't going to get in the way.

The Reverend Bodie was a nice guy. Young and good looking, so that appealed to Lyssa. He started us off with communication techniques emphasizing non-judgmental listening (sounds familiar). She told him straight away that our previous therapist had jumped the gun by suggesting she had BPD, and that's why we were looking for someone else.

After a few sessions, Lyssa told me she wanted to see him privately as well as together. I fully supported the idea.

A couple weeks later, we both sat in front of our counselor and he said, "Guys, after meeting with you together and separately, I decided to spend some time reading up on the borderline personality disorder you mentioned. I think there may be something to it."

BOOM!

Yeah, we never saw the Good Reverend again.

◆ ◆ ◆

What I Wish I Had Done

Mostly, I wish I had become more educated about BPD earlier. Even though I learned that it existed, I didn't do much reading about the symptoms, or I would have begun to connect the dots.

A few people tried to nudge us in the right direction. A social worker friend, a practicing PhD psychologist, and a ministerial counselor all considered BPD a likely cause of Lyssa's inner strife.

Only many years later did I truly acquire any skills that would have helped us communicate better. In fact, looking back on it, I was the textbook example of how *not* to react.

Use "I" Instead of "You"

I know now that when in a heated moment with a BD, it's best to respond mostly with "I" sentences instead of "you." For example:

--"I can tell you're upset because you feel I'm not willing to listen" instead of "You are making false accusations again and you need to stop."
--"I can see how angry you are" instead of "You've got nothing to be upset about."
--"I wish there was a way we could work through this" instead of "You need to calm down right now."

Stay Calm, Stay Calm, Stay the Fuck Calm

I failed miserably at remaining calm during our first few years. It got to the point where it felt like I could do nothing to keep the Crazy from taking over, so I started going with my primal instincts to defensively lash out.

If she came at me loud, I would jump back twice as loud just to shock her. It gave me a quick shot of satisfaction, but it never solved anything.

The best I came up with to stay calm was to completely ignore her. While she raged, I would simply close my eyes and project my soul to another location.

This seldom worked because it became a contest for her to provoke a response from me. She would dig at me for hours until I exploded in anger. At that point, my behavior was no better than hers.

I wish I had said things like, "I'm sure you're angry and maybe even scared. I'm feeling anger too and may not respond right now, but I'm hearing what you're saying and we can definitely talk about this later when I feel calmer."

Leave the Premises

I tried many times to leave the area when Lyssa was in rage mode. Of course, I usually did it in an angry, accusative way, saying things like, "You're nuts right now and I don't want to be anywhere around you." I had given her the opposite of what she needed. This would only trigger her desperate need to stop me from leaving.

After some bad behavior from both of us, we made a promise in front of a therapist that we wouldn't lay hands on each other in any form during an argument. She found a way to weaponize this agreement by standing in doorways when I would try to leave.

Unable to physically move her because of our agreement, I was essentially her prisoner. Once, I chose to break through a window in order to leave for work. But even if I made it to my car, there was no guarantee I'd get away. Remember, this is a woman who once jumped on the hood as I rolled out of a parking lot.

On the one occasion I chose to push her down so that I could get away from her wailing childlike actions, she had me arrested and charged with felony domestic violence. What a mess that was.

Given those scenarios, how the heck was I supposed to leave?

Calling a friend to come pick me up might have worked. I don't think Lyssa would have been willing to act out in front of a witness. But to be honest, I had allowed myself to be so isolated by Lyssa's demands, I didn't have a friend to call. Establishing a life-line pal is definitely something I should have done.

Don't Defend Against Baseless Accusations

If you're married to a BP, you have faced a litany of bizarre and untrue accusations. The natural instinct is to defend yourself, demand evidence, and offer bullet-proof responses. None of that helps or matters. It's all just noise coming from your mouth.

In fact, you may have just fallen for a ploy by your wife to distract you from an issue that was too close to the truth and triggering her fear issues. While you're babbling about an accusation, she's not listening because of her focus on what is actually consuming her mental energy at that moment.

I can't help but wonder how much time of my life was lost defending myself from Lyssa's verbal attacks. Weeks? Months?

The wasted time doesn't stop at the end of the conversation. No way. I spent hours in the coming days re-litigating everything in my head, planning what I would say the next time, like I was an attorney preparing for court (unfortunately, there was always a next time).

I wish I had learned how to say, "I can tell you believe what you just said. I'd be upset too if I thought someone did that to me. But I feel differently about it all, and I'm comfortable allowing people to believe different things. I hope you are too."

Honestly, I don't think a statement like that would have changed her mind in the least, but it would have kept me from feeling like a scolded child explaining that it wasn't me who stole a cookie.

Don't Counterattack

It became so tempting to verbally strike back at Lyssa that sometimes I gave in to base instincts. In doing so, all I did was fuel her projections of "*I'm* not the bad one, *you* are." One of our therapists referred to this brinksmanship as a surefire path to divorce: when scoring a point against the other becomes more important than staying above the fray.

Like I said, some of these techniques might work better than others, but at least you are taking control of your actions and setting standards for yourself. You may not be changing her, but you're feeling much better about the man you are. Take what you can get.

For more about unstable relationships, read on...

CHAPTER 4: UNSTABLE RELATIONSHIPS

*BPDs may display a pattern of intense and
unstable relationships with family, friends, and
loved ones.*

As we move into discussing a fourth BPD symptom, you may be noticing that there is growing overlap. Elements of "extremes" and "mood swings" also apply here. Splitting, idealization, and devaluation are also making another appearance.

This overlap and merging are part of the reason the diagnosis for BPD is difficult and has evolved over the years. Identifying a personality disorder is not a perfect science.

The *DSM-IV* stated that a diagnosis for BPD could be made if at least five of their nine symptoms were present. But what if a person had exactly five symptoms and then "recovered" from one of them? Were they no longer a BP? The *DSM-5* has tried to address this grey area, but BPD diagnosis remains challenging.

In my situation, Lyssa demonstrated clear examples of at least 10 symptoms I use in this book. An argument could be made that she mildly presented two others. Although she refused to ever be officially diagnosed with BPD, I believe it was a slam dunk.

With regard to unstable relationships, the *DSM-5* packs a lot of information into their description:

> *Intense, unstable, and conflicted close relationships, marked by mistrust, neediness, and anxious preoccupation with real or imagined abandonment; close relationships often viewed in extremes of idealization and devaluation and alternating between over involvement and withdrawal.*

They have basically combined several symptoms into one unpleasant pile of problems. If someone presents all the traits in that passage and nothing else, I'd say they have some serious problems, whether or not it can be called BPD.

Since many of these traits are being addressed in other chapters, I'll focus here on some of the new terms.

Mistrust and Neediness

During our first years of marriage, I experienced Lyssa's mistrust and neediness on many occasions. What was so challenging to me as a new husband was that these intense feelings of hers seemed to be completely unprovoked.

I hadn't committed any of the usual telltale signs of cheating or lying. No hidden bank accounts or cash fund. No unexplained hotel or restaurant receipts. No hiding my phone or secret email addresses. But in the absence of actual evidence, Lyssa would go on raids to find or create proof that her delusions were justified.

Year 1, April:

I came home from work today to be accused of being a pervert. While I was gone, she took the time to search through my entire hard drive. The reason she gave for searching "a few folders" was laughably indefensible. All she came up with was an erotic story I had downloaded before we began dating. It was located about 10 sub-folders deep and there was no way she would have "accidentally" come across it as she claimed. Yet, she tried to use it against me as evidence of some grand betrayal and misbehavior on my part. I simply blew it off, which became its own argument.

I admit that porn can be a problem in a marriage, just like any addiction. But I don't consider a little porn to be a big thing. And I certainly didn't consider one text document on an entire hard drive to be worth accusing me of deviant behavior. But that didn't stop Lyssa from mistrusting me.

What I didn't understand then is that it really didn't matter what she found on my computer. The bigger symptom on display was that while left alone all day, she began to panic that I might leave her. Her sweet angel of a husband was transitioned to a red devil.

Those feelings provoked her to attack me first, but she needed a reason. Any reason. If it wasn't the document she found, it would have been something else just as farcical.

One way or the other, I was going to be accused of being unworthy of her trust that day.

Later that year, her mistrust in me led to a much more volatile and embarrassing event. It occurred while Lyssa and I took a vacation trip to my former home state. She asked if we could attend a service at the church I had worked at for five years. I agreed, but warned her my former girlfriend and business partner, Alice, would probably be there. Here's the account from my journal:

67

Year 1, summer

For some odd reason, Lyssa made me promise that when we got to the church, I would not hug Alice. Hugging at church is pretty much standard issue, but I agreed just to keep the peace. As should have been predicted, Alice came right over and threw a big hug on me before I knew what was happening. Apparently, Lyssa was expecting me to hold out a defensive stiff arm and say, "I only hug my wife now."

As I chatted with a circle of acquaintances and introduced Lyssa, I could feel her begin to shake. She was collapsing in real-time. I excused us and took her outside where she railed on me about betraying her. This was in front of all my former work-mates and church members who looked up to me.

That was an awful day, and on our flight home I was convinced that divorce was the only outcome. She was going to be the ruin of me.

I told Lyssa that we were done and she began a full-reversal of her bad behavior. For many weeks, she was an absolute delight to be around, just like when we had started dating. Being a confirmed dumbass, I was fooled.

About a month later, I learned that Lyssa had actually committed the kind of betrayal she often accused me of. This is a prime example of projection. She just couldn't let the Alice thing go. From my journal:

Lyssa has been insisting that I contact Alice to tell her the hug didn't mean anything. I keep refusing and the arguments have been awful. Then, they abruptly stopped and she didn't bring it up again.

I discovered today that she emailed Alice from my work account and wrote all the things I refused to say, as if it was from me. Alice, bless her heart, responded with, "I can tell this isn't Rob." Alice and I aren't destined to be together, but her intuitive support in that moment is worthy of my eternal love.

Lyssa covered her tracks by deleting all copies of the email from Sent and Trash folders. If I hadn't decided to review a backup folder as I was about to delete it, I wouldn't have known.

Many years later, I spoke with Alice about the event. She said, "Knowing you so well, and having met your fragile wife that one time, I could tell it wasn't you writing those mean things." Then she hit me good with, "I just felt really sorry for you, dude."

I was a sympathy case to people whose opinions really mattered to me, and didn't even know it at the time. Pathetic.

What About Lyssa's Relationships with Her Family?

Much of the BPD literature reads as pretty tough on the parents of those with the disorder. Ample statistics are thrown around concerning the high prevalence of sexual and physical abuse. It sounds horrendous.

That's why I am happy for Lyssa in that none of those things seemed to be present in her upbringing. At least, not that I ever was told about or witnessed.

But under the trappings of a church-going, homeschooling, wholesome-living family, there was some messed up crap going on.

I spent a great deal of time around Lyssa's seven siblings, and have to say they seemed like well-adjusted and happy kids. There was an abundance of positive energy among them.

However, the story of the parents was considerably more troublesome.

They had met in the 1970s and by all appearances had adopted a groovy, hippy lifestyle, complete with a Volkswagen van converted into a camper.

As they began a family, commitments were made to raise children somewhat "off grid," free from the negative influences they saw in popular culture. No public schools, broadcast television, unsupervised computer use, or even personal radios and phones were allowed. All outside influences were to be filtered through their parental viewpoint.

Furthermore, dating and driving before age 18 was forbidden, and post-high school education would be limited. When Lyssa first announced her desire to attend college, she was directed to a storefront school with faith-based curriculum that only included content gleaned from the Bible.

Her parents believed that the girls in the family only needed enough education to be proper Christian wives who make babies.

Even years later, none of this appears sinister to my eyes, but I would certainly label it restrictive or "alternative."

The young parents soon found a church that supported these choices. The dad got a job with what would become one of the most successful computer companies in America, and the mom settled into the role of a perennially pregnant housewife and mother. After a few years, they took on the distinctive sheen of a productive, middle-class, conservative family. Go America!

Now, we fast-forward 23 years into their marriage when I came along and courted their second oldest. During that year, the family cohesion disintegrated into a fine powder.

Actually, the signs appeared a few years earlier when Lyssa's mom had resigned herself to a bedroom where she mostly slept or read. The raising of the youngest kids was abdicated to the oldest, including Lyssa. As a teen, her own youth was cut short as she was thrust into the role of sister-parent.

Then, during the summer Lyssa and I started dating, the wheels came off. Her mom first announced she wanted to separate from her husband and relocate to a spare bedroom. Then she moved to a rental house down the street. In an early sign of a daughter choosing sides, this is where Lyssa was living previous to moving in with me.

Next came the even bigger bombshell. Her mom declared she was a lesbian and would no longer hide her lifestyle.

I can only imagine the torture that woman faced for all those years, raising eight children with a husband in a deeply religious setting while rejecting the fact she was a homosexual. I would also imagine Lyssa's father feeling deeply betrayed and abandoned, as if a sacred contract had been broken.

During the ensuing divorce proceedings, I heard several details that would resonate with increased meaning later. The father fought hard in court for full custody of the kids, declaring that their mother had mental problems and couldn't be a trusted caretaker.

This made Lyssa fume, and she forever blamed her father for making false accusations. No, the irony was not lost on me.

On another occasion, Lyssa's mom admitted that their grand experiment in child rearing was an abject failure. Her wish to raise the younger kids differently than they had the oldest was partially responsible for her depression and reclusiveness.

I was present when Lyssa received an apology from her mom for decades of misguided parenting. Lyssa must have felt devastated to hear, "We totally botched it raising you that way. Sorry." Not exactly a self-esteem builder.

So, is Lyssa's family history obviously the root cause of her borderline personality disorder? I would say the crushingly strict way her parents sheltered the kids definitely played a role. But it was Lyssa who completed the actions initiated by others.

For instance, what her parents considered proper media oversight, Lyssa mutated into a gangly, soul-smashing war against her perception of porn and sexuality.

Mind you, these were issues she only held *me* accountable for, not herself. Never once did she come home declaring dread that she had unwillingly beheld a seductive billboard. Only if *I* had seen such a thing was there a problem.

Secondly, the clandestine lesbian identity of her mother and the father's vengeful accusations of mental disorder is too blatant to ignore as an influence on Lyssa.

Basically, what Lyssa witnessed was a woman hiding a central core of her personality from her husband under the profound fear that he would shame her and strip away the most important elements of her self-identity (the children). Which is exactly what happened.

So yeah, considering what I've learned about BPD, I'd say there's a connection.

But it's not a smoking gun. Lyssa's siblings, especially the older ones, did not display any BPD symptoms.

During a particularly rough patch, I reached out to Lyssa's older sister for advice, and she gave me a respectful but mostly reserved response. It was clear to me she didn't think I was being honest.

I had thought that if anyone in the family was aware of BPD-like traits in Lyssa's past, it would be her closest sister. She really had no clue.

In hindsight (there's that damn word again), it's obvious there was also a connection between the way Lyssa felt about her father and me. From her perspective, he was an overbearing narcissist who didn't trust his wife and tried to control the actions of all those around him.

She first turned to me as a savior. I could rescue her from the pater's domination and steal her away to a life of love and prosperity.

I was only too happy to buy into the façade. Men like me love to be the heroes.

Of course, as soon as she was liberated, she assigned to me all of her father's worst attributes. He and I were suddenly the same person. She once screamed at me, "This is a nightmare. How did I let this happen *again*?"

What I Wish I Had Done:
People with BPD are prone to enter quickly into romantic relationships. As is their wont, they view a new suitor as an angel of delight. They see only the good and surely in this person, they will find all the love they seek.

Even as an older and supposedly wiser man, I was caught up in the romance of her affections for me. There in front of me was a charming, cute, talented woman telling me I was everything she has dreamt of. I, and only I, would be the one to sweep her away.

In return, I was the recipient of boundless praise, shoulder rubs, steamy sex, and all-around pleasant company. It seemed like a pretty good deal to me.

She moved into my house within a few weeks. After a couple months, I invited her to relocate out of state to make a life together, and we were married about eight months after our first date. It was all so wicked fast...and exciting.

Looking back (see how I avoided saying "hindsight?"), I should have applied the brakes and looked at the relationship as if it was happening to a best friend.

Perhaps I would have given more weight to her emotional frailness, her regular bouts of crying, and her peculiarities about "adult content" that I didn't view as particularly adult.

Would that have led to me ultimately not marrying her? Probably not. You know how it is when you first fall in love. Everything is *grand*. For the first time in your life you know exactly what you want, so you don't want to waste another minute without taking action.

But slowing down the pace of our relationship still would have been the right choice. At least I could have said, "I took my time, and it didn't matter anyway. The Crazy would have stayed hidden whether it took a month or a year."

Sometimes, I suspect Lyssa's father knew more than he let on. Perhaps he was privy to a husband's insight regarding his own wife's mental state. Was she a BP? Possibly, but no one ever used the term in front of me.

What is known is that he soon limited any unsupervised visits with Lyssa and the younger siblings. This was a blatant statement on his part that by choosing to take her mother's side, she was going to face consequences.

Was he a controlling S.O.B. as Lyssa said, or was he simply protecting his youngest children from the same traits and behavior he had already seen in his wife? I'm sure he'll never say.

We'll explore more about the distorted self-image of a BP in a moment, but first, **I have a favor to ask...**

PASS IT ON

If you're finding this book useful, I'd be very grateful if you'd **post an honest review** with Amazon. The more reviews, the higher the chances others who need the book will see it.

To leave a review, all you need to do is visit the book's Amazon page. Scroll down and you'll see a button/link that says "Write a customer review" – click on that and you're good to go. While you're at the page, please "follow" me as an author so you'll be notified about future books.

Thank you for the support,
~Robert

In the eBook, you may click/tap here to leave a review.

Tell Me Your Story!

I'd love to hear from you. Join the Facebook support group, Roses and Rage: Spouses of Borderline Personality Disorder, to share your experiences. I would especially love to hear from spouses who have found ways to reduce the BPD problems in your relationship.

Now, let's continue...

CHAPTER 5: DISTORTED SELF-IMAGE

BPDs may display a distorted and unstable self-image or sense of self

Let's see what the *DSM-5* adds to the description of this trait:

> *Markedly impoverished, poorly developed, or unstable self-image, often associated with excessive self-criticism; chronic feelings of emptiness; dissociative states under stress.*

As we discussed earlier, this is a difficult symptom for the non-BP to grasp. I know I often asked myself, "How the heck can a person not think they exist?" Followed by, "All they have to do is look in the mirror and say hello."

My lack of understanding allowed me yet another reason to not fully accept borderline personality disorder as a real thing in my marriage. It just didn't seem possible that an intelligent and talented person like Lyssa could be *that* messed up.

On this particular issue, *I* was the one who was messed up because I didn't ask more questions and educate myself. I'll try to keep you from repeating my mistakes.

Lacking a concise self-image, a BP will seek out others to fill the emptiness. If your wife has BPD, part of the reason she is attracted to you is your strong self-identity. She sees it as worthy of co-opting for her own. Through you, she can feel more comfortable in her existence. In *I Hate You—Don't Leave Me: Understanding the Borderline Personality Disorder*, authors Jerold Kreisman and Hal Straus explain it in theatrical terms:

> *To overcome their indistinct and mostly negative self-image, borderlines, like actors, are constantly searching for "good roles," complete "characters" they can use to fill their identity void.*

While you and I fully formed a sense of self by our young-adult years, the BP has to keep searching.

According to *Stop Walking on Eggshells*, BPs commonly report feeling:

--there is "nothing to me"
--they are different people depending on who they are with
--that being alone leaves them without a sense of self
--they are dependent on others for cues about how to behave, what to think, and how to be

To help relate these feelings to your own situation, let's explore them one at a time with real-life examples.

"Nothing to me:"
During one of Lyssa's several impassioned declarations that she wanted to kill herself, she screamed at me, "The ONLY reason I'm not doing it right now is because of what it would do to my little sister."

She was referring to the sister assigned to her to raise when their mom became too depressed for the task.

But take note of where she placed the emphasis. She saw no life-saving value from her marriage to a loving husband, plans for a family, goals as an artist, or even impending academic achievements—all moments most of us hold up as self-defining benchmarks. In the depths of her despair, they meant nothing to her.

The only flicker of hope she could cling to in that dreadful moment was the self-image of an innocent child, and I'm glad she did.

BPs are different people depending on who they are with:
BPs have the ability to bend their personalities in chameleon-like fashion. This is *not* the same thing as having multiple personalities. Rather, it's the BP navigating the world without a strong sense of self, so they temporarily latch onto whatever "self" happens to be handy.

This leads to great frustration for the spouse of a BP. We fulfill a singular role in eyes of our wife, so as a BP, she treats us much differently than most of the people she interacts with. We get to see her absolute best *and* worst in extremes that no one else is aware of.

When the day comes that we feel compelled to seek help or advice from friends and family, all we are likely to receive is doubt and raised eyebrows. Common responses are, "Oh, you must be exaggerating. You guys are a great couple and so much in love," or "I've known her even longer than you, and I don't think we're talking about the same person."

This disconnect resulted in me usually keeping my mouth shut. If I did speak up, I came off as provoking and outlandish. People would apply stereotypes, turning me into the manipulative husband, while my wife was the innocent victim in need of protection from a brute.

Combined with Lyssa's other actions to isolate us from outside connections, I often felt unable to discuss our problems with anyone. That's a depressing place to find oneself.

I don't believe Lyssa was actively deceiving anyone by "changing" to fit who she was with. She was just using a coping method in the face of not having a strong enough sense of self to rely on across all situations.

Being alone leaves the BP without a sense of self:
As you can imagine, since a BP requires others to bulk up their own sense of self, they become particularly desperate when there aren't others around to fill the empty spaces.

I lost count of all the times Lyssa pleaded with me not to leave her alone during arguments or her "anxiety attacks" (as she called her BPD-related episodes). She became especially panic-ridden if I was leaving to be with other people. This was a double-punch to her worst fears. Not only would she be alone, but her husband was out realizing he could have a better life without her.

A couple months before we were married, I flew to my home state for a high-school reunion. We decided it would be too expensive for her to come with me and that we should save the money towards our honeymoon.

During the event, Lyssa went on a calling binge, reaching out to me every 15-20 minutes, essentially ruining my interaction with former classmates. I had to excuse myself from every conversation to spend 10 minutes calming Lyssa down and refuting her accusations that I was misbehaving.

Being home alone, Lyssa suffered from several BPD symptoms simultaneously: lack of self-identity, fear of abandonment, "splitting" me from a trusted boyfriend into a philandering rogue, and a desperate sense of emptiness.

I assumed I was simply paying the price for dating a younger woman who needed "a little" extra reassurance. Meanwhile, she was suffering from a thousand demons swirling in her head. I had no idea what she was going through.

Dependent on others for cues about how to behave, what to think, and how to be:

This takes me back to the moment Lyssa and I returned from our honeymoon. Being tired, I decided to take an afternoon nap, to which she replied, with great agitation in her voice, "But what am I supposed to do?"

That was one of the oddest questions I had ever been asked. Why would me napping have any bearing whatsoever on Lyssa doing whatever the heck she wanted?

It's reminiscent to a young child surrounded by toys but turning to a parent and saying, "There's nothing to do. I'm bored!" In that case, the parent will probably feel obliged to suggest activities or interact with the child.

I was hearing the same kind of frustration coming from the mouth of a grown woman. Yet, she expected me to entertain her just as I might a bored little girl.

Among child psychologists, there is a school of thought that says infants consider whatever is outside their field of vision to not exist. Things and people simply vanish and reappear. The infant can only conceive of the world immediately in front of them.

With a BP, it is not everyone else who disappears when out of the room, it is themselves. That's a terrifying concept. A BP might ask, "If a tree falls in the forest and I'm the only one to hear it, do I exist?"

When Lyssa asked, "What shall I do?" what she meant was, "What will happen to me?"

She became incredibly dependent upon me to give her world meaning and substance. This made me feel grandly self-important. I suppose it triggered some sense of masculine satisfaction to believe my wife couldn't thrive without me. But the problem was much deeper and unhealthier than I knew at the time.

What I hope you're beginning to grasp with all this discussion about lack of self-identity is that I understand how difficult it is to believe it is a real thing. But if you're ever going to have any empathy and understanding for the BP in your life, you must embrace that *she* believes. Period.

What I Wish I Had Done:
A couple days after my botched high-school reunion, I wrote an entry in my journal describing the conclusion of that night. I had gotten tired of Lyssa calling me repeatedly and here's how I dealt with it:

I finally said, "I'm done with these calls. You're trying to ruin my night. I will call you later when I'm done here." As it turns out, an attractive woman at the reunion did invite me to her hotel room, but I declined. When I eventually called Lyssa, she said she was miserable all night because I was so selfish and insensitive. It was already very late and I had a 6 am flight, so I told her whatever she needed to hear just to get off the phone.

Did you catch that last bit? I set a terrible precedent there by telling her "whatever she needed." In that moment, I totally screwed myself and didn't do Lyssa any favors either.

I spent the following years repeating that misstep by falsely expressing agreement with Lyssa in order to "get:" *get* off the phone, *get* some sleep, *get* to work, etc. I have no doubt that Lyssa learned to manipulate me by dredging up a problem just as I was about to "get."

One of our therapists suggested we promise not to bring up any potentially difficult topics after 8 pm. I whole heartedly agreed. But in practice Lyssa couldn't stop herself. The Crazy simply wouldn't leave her in peace as we would lie in bed.

I'd be quietly reading a hobby-related magazine about music or sports and she would interject: "Why do you always have to read articles about women?"

I had learned that whenever she used demonstrative words like "always" or "never," we were doomed. There would be no talking to her about that particular topic. Because, as I only learned much later, the topic was never what she was actually talking about.

I now know that whenever a BP confronts you about something that on face value seems random and ridiculous, it's related somehow to fear of abandonment and losing the one thing that provides them self-identity. But rather than be able to express that fear, the BP will simply attack you with baseless accusations.

My intuition about how to react to Lyssa seemed to completely fail me. Like most of us would, I turned to defensiveness and logic, which is useless when dealing with a BP in panic mode. You can't logically defend your way out of a situation when it isn't actually the situation.

Even if you make yourself breathless presenting a full-proof argument that you are innocent of her accusation, she will have already moved on to another that is even more preposterous. The list never gets shorter my friend.

So basically, what I wish I had done is the opposite of everything I did. Simple, right?

There is a classic *Seinfeld* episode where George Costanza decides that since his life has not gone the direction he hoped, he would now only do the opposite of what his instincts told him. Sure enough, his life immediately improved, despite going against his logic.

I should have been more like George.

In *When Words Hurt, How to Keep Criticism from Undermining Your Self-Esteem*, Mary Lynne Heldmann writes about the Four Don'ts: don't deny, don't defend, don't counterattack, and don't withdraw.

Rather than denying or defending, I should have asked reaffirming questions like, "Can you tell me why the thought of what you're saying upsets you so much?"

Rather than attacking Lyssa with equal force, I should have remained calm in the knowledge that it's not ever really about me. The root cause to nearly every accusation was Lyssa's fear of being alone and disappearing.

Rather than withdraw by clamming up and ignoring her when she tried to start a fight before bedtime, I should have found a way to say, "I can tell this is important to you, so it's important to me too, and I'm not going anywhere. Let me think about what you're saying tonight and we'll talk about it at breakfast."

Would these techniques all have worked in most situations? Doubtful. But it's ultimately not about changing the behavior of a BP. We can hope for such things, but not expect them. Instead, we have to be content with changes in our own behavior that give us a stronger feeling of self-respect and authenticity.

Simply telling a BP "what they need" is only a short-term fix, because they probably need the exact opposite. Be like George.

Who Doesn't love Animals?

Here it is: the tale I'm the most woeful to share. I'm still disgusted with my choices. Above all else, this was the test I so dreadfully failed. An innocent soul depended on me for protection. There can be no forgiveness.

I had a cat. Which was odd, because I never liked cats. He was a neighborhood drifter, fed by a few but owned by none. He began hanging around my open door until one day he never left. Ringer, as I named him, simply chose not to leave, and I agreed to the arrangement by not saying no.

When Lyssa moved with me to my new job, she knew that meant we'd have Ringer in the picture. He was my cat. That's how life works. She was now a cat parent.

Living in our new apartment, Ringer became an indoor cat for the first time, and he handled it like a champ with no complaints. Lyssa, on the other hand, began showing several signs of cat-related stress.

"Why does he always stare at me? Make him stop." I'd scratch my head and respond, "Um, he's a cat Lyssa, I don't think there's much to it." She later added, "He watches me when I'm naked and I don't like it."

Then the jealously kicked in. "Why do you ALWAYS have to give him attention instead of me?" When I'd say that cats need to be looked after, she'd fire back, "It's stupid you care so much. You're just being manipulated."

When I once expressed that I actually loved the little guy, she was furious. "You can't really love an animal! You're just being taken advantage of by a stupid cat who wants you to feed him!"

And it's not that Lyssa was an adamant "dog person." I learned later she didn't like them either.

I soon found myself making concessions as to how often I could spend time with Ringer, because Lyssa considered that time away from her, even if we were in the room together.

It got worse.

In the coming weeks, I noticed she would scare Ringer into hiding behind a kitchen cabinet where I couldn't get to him and offer comfort. She smiled when it happened. It amused her.

What was wrong with her? Who doesn't like animals?

The fights continued. Ringer was the poor victim of his parent's division. Her accusations of me being a terrible husband became relentless. "How could you love that animal more than me? What's wrong with you? Can't you see I'm miserable? I'm physically sick with it around. If you loved me, you'd do something about my health and get rid of the problem!"

In a moment I've never forgotten, I caught Lyssa smacking Ringer in the head for no reason. I blew up at her and announced, "From this moment on, any attack on him is an attack on me, and I will respond accordingly. You hit him, I hit you." She was stunned. "You're choosing the stupid cat over me?"

Was I? I guess it was true. What kind of husband wouldn't save his wife from her anguish when all it would take is getting rid of a cat? I mean, I don't even like cats. You can get them free anywhere. They have no *value*. What the hell am I waiting for? Prove to your wife how much you love her and get rid of "the problem."

Unsure, I came up with a test. I told Lyssa I would find Ringer another home but that I felt sure this act would forever damage our marriage. Without waiting a beat, she swiftly agreed with those terms.

That's the moment of clarity I had been waiting for! Her mental sickness was undeniable and the only choice was to gather up my things and head off to greener pastures with my pal Ringer and self-respect well in hand. I would get rid of the problem alright—my wife.

I waited for a day she was out of the apartment for several hours, loaded up my truck and bailed on the crazy cat-hater. Fuck that nut-job. Life got better the minute I pulled the trigger and never looked back.

Yeah, none of that happened. I gave the cat away.

Lyssa quickly placed five more things on the list of my husband-shortcomings.

Pathetic. Loser. Couldn't. Even. Protect. An. Innocent. Cat.

CHAPTER 6: IMPULSIVE BEHAVIORS

*Impulsive and often dangerous behaviors, such as
spending sprees, unsafe sex, substance abuse,
reckless driving, and binge eating*

Having read about the kinds of impulsive behaviors others have faced with a BP spouse, I feel fortunate my experiences weren't so devastating. Online support groups are rife with stories of financial ruin, drug overdoses, alcohol abuse, and unplanned pregnancies from affairs. Why are those things so prevalent with BPs?

According to the *DSM-5*, impulsivity is described as:

> *Acting on the spur of the moment in response to immediate stimuli; acting on a momentary basis without a plan or consideration of outcomes; difficulty establishing or following plans; a sense of urgency and self-harming behavior under emotional distress.*

It's easy to imagine those traits being highly destructive to a relationship. How would you react to find your wife had smashed yet another car, drained the savings account on a gambling spree, maxed out a credit card you didn't even know about, or tells you she's pregnant by another man and it's your fault for not being a better husband?

These are all-too-common experiences for men married to a BP. In *I Hate You—Don't Leave Me*, the authors say, "The borderline's behaviors may be sudden and contradictory, since they result from strong, momentary feelings." They add, "The immediacy of the present exists in isolation, without the benefit of the experience of the past, or the hopefulness of the future."

For the BP caught up in this symptom, **there is no before or after**, only now, and the now is often distressing. With no reference points across a spectrum of time, the BP has little reason to not live for the moment. Sometimes those moments are quite destructive.

You and I will consider what we've learned from previous experiences and factor in likely consequences before commencing an impulsive act. I might think, "I'd like to take my whole pay check and bet it on one horse race, just for the thrill." But then my inhibitors kick in: "I suppose I had better pay for the rent and my kid's medicine instead."

With less ability to view the before and after, a BP is much more likely than I am to say, "This is fun. Bet it all!" To make matters even worse, after the BP comes down from the high of their impulsive actions, they tend to underrate the gravity of what happened.

While you're left to mop up a catastrophic mess, your wife is saying, "I don't know what the big deal is."

I can't help but think it's no coincidence that one of Lyssa's favorite movies is called *Memento* from 2001. The protagonist suffers a head trauma and is no longer able to retain short-term memories. Each day he must re-create his post-trauma life through a series of polaroid photographs and post-it notes. Knowing his recent past will soon be forgotten and his eventual future will form no permanent memories, he exists perpetually in the current moment.

BPs act in a similar fashion with devasting results for the non-BP spouse. Each time the BP goes on a bender of impulsivity, it is the spouse who feels like they have to be the parent in the relationship, always saying things like, "Now honey, you probably shouldn't do that."

Besides the momentary thrill, the BP might also be using impulsivity to fill the emptiness of their self-identity crisis. A BP would much rather fill the time with heart-racing thrills than be alone facing the fear of abandonment and non-existence.

For those caught in the wake of an impulsive BP, life is *temporarily* a total blast. Maybe that's how you met your wife. It could happen like this:

You're at a friend's wedding reception and you see an attractive woman calling out for more drinks. She sways seductively to the music, flirts with men surrounding her, but then sets her eyes on you. The rest of the night is a blur of alcohol, dirty dancing, party drugs, and risky-but-awesome sex.

You're in love!

If you're lucky, you find out in the morning she's already married and your common sense prevails. You never see her again.

Or, she is equally as entranced. She says she's never been so attracted to any man and is sure you are the soul mate she's been waiting her whole life to find. A thrilling romance ensues and you are married before the year is out.

Only then does she begin to show you the other traits of BPD she has lived with her whole life but are brand new to you. Her fears take over, she attacks you with inexplicable accusations, you are the last man on earth who can make her happy, she screams at you to leave her alone, and then screams at you when you do.

Soon, the pendulum swings, and you're once again the angel in the morning to your doting and appreciate wife.

Proving the Impossible

In her BPD memoir *Girl in Need of a Tourniquet*, Merri Lisa Johnson beautifully describes what she would want to see a lover do to prove their love:

> *I will call your name in public for all the world to hear and they will know I love you and you will know it and all manner of things will be well.*

Demonstrating the immense difficulty in trying to convince a BP they are loved, she goes on to say, "I picture it tattooed in a trail down my spine. I need the message to mean something. I need it to be real."

Lyssa became obsessed with finding new ways for me to prove I loved her. The failures always outweighed the victories.

Once, she ran out of the house crying and distraught. She came back hours later, exhausted and dehydrated. She said she had walked the length of a highway and bridge nearby that I knew had no room for pedestrian traffic. When I asked why she didn't walk a safer route, she replied, "You were supposed to come stop me before I got there."

On the occasions I tried to get away during an argument, it was to defuse a volatile situation and give us both time apart. When she was the one to leave, I was supposed to chase after her, proclaiming my great love and needfulness. All these rules were apparently written down somewhere, but I never found where they were kept.

Another test she came up with proved to be very expensive. She announced that she needed to move out for a while so that "we could both do some thinking." I knew that was code for "*you* need to do better."

We found her a studio rental, paid three times the rent to get her moved in, and bought all the necessities to set up her life there. Six weeks later she was ready to move back home. "You never came over to try and win me back" she protested.

"Hey Robert! Whatever happened with that story about being in jail?"

Ah yes, good question. After meeting with an attorney, it was suggested the best path for me was to plead guilty to felony domestic violence with a request for court-mandated counseling. The other option was to fight the charges in an expensive trial and try to convince the court I had a wife with a mental disorder. I went with the first suggestion.

It turns out that the mandated counseling was better known as "anger management" classes run by an approved therapist. In order to have the verdict expunged, I would need to complete six months of weekly classes. There were only two choices for locations, so I picked the one closer to home.

This brings us to...

Therapist #3 (Anger Management, part 1)

After arriving at my anger management meeting place, I thought the building looked familiar. When I went inside and took a seat, I knew why...the therapist was Doctor Duck!

I was relieved. He had seemed like a good guy and maybe these classes wouldn't be too unpleasant. He recognized me and invited me to tell my story to the group. After I explained how I arrived there due to a BP wife and my lack of knowing how to cope, he simply said, "Yup, welcome to the party."

When I got home that night, Lyssa naturally wanted to know how things went. I told her who my therapist was and she flipped out. The very next day she was at the courthouse insisting they switch me to another class where the therapist "wasn't on his side." She actually made it happen. I got reassigned by the end of the day.

You see, Lyssa was still under the impression that *I* was the one with the problem. In her mind, I was the same narcissistic, verbally abusive, control freak as her father.

She was convinced that if I learned how control my anger, everything else in our relationship would be okay. The possibility that she suffered from a severe personality disorder didn't come into the picture.

I, on the other hand, didn't think I had any anger problems that weren't a direct result of her BPD behavior and was only attending the classes to get the whole mess expunged without a trial.

So, it was goodbye Doctor Duck, and hello to...

Therapist #4 (Anger Management, part 2)

The new group therapist I was assigned to for anger management was well-intentioned but woefully under skilled for the job. It was clear that she just looked at it as a government paycheck to keep the office lights on.

Each week, Lyssa would ask me what I learned in class. I'm sure she was hoping for some advanced meditation or mindfulness techniques that would allow me to stop ruining our marriage. But instead, my completely honest answers included:

--We sat around and colored
--We gave each other shoulder rubs
--We drew pictures of tress
--We drew pictures of birds
--We shared the names of good divorce attorneys
--We talked about whether or not we could still own hunting rifles before our convictions were expunged

Lyssa was not at all pleased with the quality of my therapy. She found it unsettling that I didn't seem to be making strides against the tide of my supposed anger. I reminded her who insisted on getting me switched to a different therapist. In a rare act of contrition, she stayed quiet.

◆ ◆ ◆

Facing the judicial system due to my wife's BPD was an abysmal education for me. There were no allowances for what was really going on.

My naiveté was definitely a handicap as I got moved from one level of the system to another. I was clueless and very much at the mercy of others.

When Lyssa made her original complaint at the sheriff's office, there was no one questioning her authenticity or mental clarity. When the officers came to arrest me, they didn't ask about a family history of mental health. There was no check box for "My wife imprisoned me and made it impossible for me to leave without touching her." It was simply, "Did you push her? Okay then, you're under arrest."

When I faced the judge, there was no exception for degrees. A mild push was considered the same assault as a punch in the face. No discussion. Send me away and bring in the next case. Plead guilty or spend your life savings going to trial.

At the anger management classes, I sat surrounded by men who had been black-out drunk, crashed cars through living-room walls, threatened family members with loaded shotguns, and attempted suicide by cop. Yet, we were all found guilty of the exact same crime and sentenced to the same punishment.

To avoid pleading guilty the way I did, I would have needed to hire a team of attorneys and psychological experts, and find several friends and family members willing to testify that Lyssa had a history of mental problems and false accusations. I did not have the resources or the heart for such a battle that would tear my wife down in public.

What I can tell you from first-hand experience is that the court system is not designed to be understanding to the spouses of BPD. You will not come through the other side without losing some combination of wealth, time, self-respect, and the respect of others.

Two words: avoid it.

CHAPTER 7: SELF-HARM

BPDs may display self-harming behavior, such as cutting

The vast majority of BPD symptoms are only witnessed by immediate family and friends of the BP. The circle of acquaintances outside that group might have no awareness of the disorder in their midst. But with acts of self harm, the signs become more external and difficult to ignore.

The *DSM-IV* describes the self-harm symptom as, "Recurrent suicidal behavior, gestures, or threats, or self-mutilating behavior." Notice how suicide and self-harm are bound together. This was later viewed as less helpful and led to a revision in the *DSM-5*:

> *Engagement in dangerous, risky, and potentially self-damaging activities, unnecessarily and without regard to consequences; lack of concern for one's limitations and denial of the reality of personal danger.*

The term "self-harm" is replaced with "risk taking" and "self-damaging activities." The unnerving aspect is "without regard to consequences." Without a strong sense of past or future, a BP will see no problem with harming themselves in the present. Like so many actions of the BP, consequences are simply not a factor.

The types of self-harm associated with BP behavior may include:

--cutting
--skin scratching
--head banging
--hair pulling
--tearing off scabs
--needle poking
--burning
--biting
--breaking bones

The authors of *Stop Walking on Eggshells* add this:

> *Sometimes, dangerous or compulsive behavior can be a type of self-mutilation—overeating to the point of obesity, for example, or provoking physical fights with others.*

So, why would a BP choose to hurt themselves? It's mostly a coping mechanism. If a BP feels numb and without a self-identity, pain is a method to feel alive or "real."

In her memoir, *Girl in Need of a Tourniquet*, Merri Lisa Johnson disturbingly describes her self-harm as a message of self-loathing: "I want to tell them I carve scarlet letters in my skin like hate mail in the dead letter office of my body."

For me, the thought of being physically hurt *causes* stress. For a BP, it *releases* stress. They are able to focus on the pain and therefore find temporary relief from emotional hurt or frustration.

In fact, self-harm as coping can even be performed unconsciously. The BP feels stress and simply initiates a behavior to relieve the anxiety, without knowing they are doing so.

Conversely, a BP might engage in self-harm as a means to ask others for help. I know this was the case with Lyssa. She wasn't admitting to BPD, but she certainly used self-harm as a means to say, "I'm in a desperate situation here."

I often wondered how an intelligent woman like Lyssa could engage in self-harm without having to admit something was terribly wrong with her emotions. But she seemed to do it in a way that was either impulsive or unconscious and therefore "not of her own doing." She intellectually knew what she had done, but disowned herself of the responsibility.

Here is a journal entry that refers to an early sign of self-harm in our marriage:

Year 1, July:
I asked L why both her thumbs seemed so irritated and raw. She acted like she wasn't aware and dismissed the question. I see her picking at them while we watch TV, so I know she's doing it to herself. I think it started during final exams, but it hasn't stopped.

I was somewhat correct in associating her self-harming behavior with the stress of her school. But of course, the causes were more pervasive than I knew at that time. It was always about the BPD.

Rather than view her actions as part of a larger problem, I wrote it off as a "normal" thing people might do and no big deal. I mean, who wants to admit their new wife might not be normal, right?

Over the years, the incidents of self-harm in my marriage became more pronounced and varied.

I spotted a few cut marks on her arms and would ask her what had happened. "Oh, that," she'd say. "I guess I nicked myself somehow. I forget how it happened." The marks were always small enough that her response was plausible. I grew up in a house with brothers and we were always ending up with scraps and scabs without knowing how.

A completely undeniable act of self-harm was noted in a later journal entry:

Year 2, December
Last night we had a terrible fight that began with her insisting I never watch movies when she's not home. I told her that "was nuts" and refused. She exploded into a rage and launched various accusations at me about not loving her. At the height of her anger, she demanded that I apologize and comfort her. I said, "You got yourself this mad, you can get yourself calm again." She looked around the room as if she was searching for something to hurt me with. Instead, she ran full speed at the wall and lowered her head just as she hit. She stumbled back and did it again even harder. This time she collapsed to the floor and cried, "See what you made me do."

I felt horrible inner conflict at that moment. Had I really made her do that? Should I have agreed to what she asked to keep it from happening? My poor wife had just tried to knock herself out and I just stood there watching it happen.

I sat with her on the floor and held her, offering the comfort she craved. But in my mind, I was repulsed. Who (or what) had I married?

There was nothing about what I had just witnessed that I could spin as normal. My wife was clearly *not* okay.

Whether she did it consciously or not, Lyssa had finally "outed" herself in a way that was undeniable. Her action screamed out to me, "I'M IN DANGER!" Unfortunately, her plea was still couched in, "AND IT'S YOUR FAULT!"

♦ ♦ ♦

Let me return to the events around the time of my anger management classes. During these months, I was absolutely convinced that divorce was the likely outcome. I hated the thought of it, but felt I was left with little choice.

This wife of mine had put me in jail for a ludicrous reason. I could only imagine what she'd have to do the next time in order to top herself. Would she commit suicide in a way that framed me for her death? Would she kill me before taking her own life? Nothing seemed off the table at that point.

My visit with a divorce attorney was not reassuring. Divorce laws in that southern state were purposefully draconian. By making divorce both difficult and lengthy, people were less likely to abandon a marriage. The process required a 1-year separation supported by the testimony of a friend affirming that the married couple had not had sex during that time.

The only exception to the waiting period was a declaration of physical abuse. False imprisonment, baseless accusations, and having a spouse put in jail for bogus reasons didn't qualify. It was throwing punches or nothing.

But as far as Lyssa knew, I was committed to divorce and gathering information. I even looked for another place to live and went as far as putting down a deposit.

As often happens with BPs, she saw she had gone too far and immediately reversed her behavior. She managed to put a muzzle on the Crazy for quite a while.

Lyssa's fear of loneliness kicked into high gear and she swore things would be better for us. Although, she still seemed to think the biggest improvements would stem from the skills I would learn in anger management classes and less from any long-term changes she would make.

Nonetheless, she modulated her behavior and became a once-again nice person to be around. We returned to the simple activities that gave us joy like playing board games, making meals together, and talking about future plans.

The self-harm behaviors disappeared, and I very much enjoyed seeing her again as the joyful woman I had married. Lyssa could really be charming, sexy, and downright pleasant. I truly missed that side of her.

She eventually turned the conversation to me giving up on any ideas of moving out and getting a divorce. I saw an opportunity.

I had been reading the literature given to us by therapists along the way and started to see the strong correlation between our life and traits of borderline personality disorder. As I would move down the list of symptoms, it read like a bullet-point outline of our problems.

I came up with a plan that I assume will make all BPD therapists cringe and shake their heads: in exchange for me staying in the marriage, Lyssa would have to allow me to read the entire BPD pamphlet to her without making any comment until the end.

Much to my surprise, she agreed.

Yeah, it did not go well.

At the conclusion of each symptom, I would turn to her and pause before moving on. I'm sure my silence only screamed at her, "SEE! I TOLD YOU IT WAS ALL YOUR FAULT!"

I could sense her seething with anger and resentment. But, honoring her agreement, she let me finish, and I stopped pursuing a divorce. However, she never forgave me for the humiliation.

I don't blame her. I do think my primary motivation was one of caring for her, to open the door to her seeking help, but she was not prepared to face such a monumental admission.

It was too similar to what her father had done to wrest child custody away from her mother. He had made their troubles all his wife's fault, and in her depressed state she was unwilling to fight the charges in the divorce settlement.

Now, there I was fulfilling her accusations that I was a controlling narcissist just like her father. I saw an opportunity to force a BPD self-diagnosis on her and took it. That was not appropriate, and I regret the event.

We remained married, but our trust in each other took a big hit. I couldn't trust if she was truly in my corner or just waiting for a chance to make me pay. And she had to wonder if I would ever take responsibility for any bad behavior when I could simply blame it on her personality disorder.

The arguing soon returned. The Crazy was back with fortified resolve. I'm sure she thought, "How dare he make me hear those nasty false accusations. He's trying to control me instead of loving me for who I am."

At one point during this period, she angrily pushed me off a chair to the floor. When I asked how it was acceptable that I had been put in jail for a similar act, she had no response. Someone with no past or future can't grasp facing consequences for their actions.

Around this timeframe, I had developed a full list of defenses against her mood swings. They are described in this journal entry where I went on a bit of a rant:

Year 3, October:
Her accusing me of some misbehavior when we are in public has become common enough that I now always carry extra cash with me in case I need to leave and find a way home. I'm also hiding extra housekeys around the yard for the same reason. We've stopped shopping together because of magazines and posters with women featured. Movies are out because I can't control if a triggering scene might pop up. Most TV shows I liked are out too. We are limited to basically watching Shrek *videos, sports without women, and PBS.*

I had heard for years about women who carried a "fuck-you twenty" in their purse on a date, just in case they needed to bail out. There I was, doing the same thing, but with my wife.

During arguments, it was common for me to walk into our yard to get away from her, which might be followed by her locking the door behind me.

I usually enjoyed the peace and quiet as she "punished" me, but there were a few times I needed to get to appointments and she wouldn't unlock the door. Thus, I had several extra keys tucked around the yard so that I could get into my house.

As for watching sports, I had spent my young-adult years living in a coastal community where beach volleyball was popular and I had often played. When the Summer Olympics featured the beach volleyball event, I thought nothing of watching those amazing athletes do their thing.

Lyssa attacked me with, "Why do you have to watch those women in their trashy swim suits?" My response was, "How about you watch the men play in their trashy swimsuits and we call it a day?" Yeah, that didn't go over well.

The thought of her watching hunky dudes didn't bother me in the least because I had a strong sense of self. She, on the other hand, jumped directly from me looking at a female athlete's legs to, "He will leave me to have sex with her and I'll cease to exist."

When faced with such a disparity of views, there really isn't any room for compromise. Something like, "I'll just watch for 20 minutes and you'll only cease to exist until lunch" just doesn't compute. But this is how far apart we were on what was such a small concern to me.

With Lyssa, there was never a *small* disagreement. Her day quickly went from, "Sure, let's watch some of the Olympics," to "This is the WORST day of my life and you're an awful husband," as she began pulling at the cuticles of her thumbs.

What I Wish I Had Done:

I totally botched it when I insisted Lyssa review all the symptoms of BPD with me. In my frustration, I went too far, too soon. But there might still have been a way to leverage her needs into positive actions.

I wish I had used the situation to achieve a smaller, more manageable goal. When she asked that I give up on divorce and moving out, I could have said:

> "That's something we can talk about because I don't want to leave you. I still care about you and our marriage, but sometimes I'm upset by what I see. Do you think we could try a new counselor together and I could talk about what makes me upset and you could ask about the sores on your fingers and arms?"

That tactic might have worked. It would have hit on her belief that my anger was the big problem, while giving her aircover to talk about self-harming behavior that was clearly taking place.

Self-harm is bad enough, but read on for a discussion of suicidal behavior.

CHAPTER 8: SUICIDE

BPDs may display recurring thoughts of suicidal behaviors or threats

Of all the BPD traits I faced with Lyssa, suicidal threats were the scariest. I had no training or experience with what I was confronted by and failed miserably at being helpful. Maybe I can help others avoid similar mistakes by sharing what I learned.

As for the *DSM-5*, they group suicide together with other symptoms as such:

> *Frequent feelings of being down, miserable, and/or hopeless; difficulty recovering from such moods; pessimism about the future; pervasive shame; feelings of inferior self-worth; thoughts of suicide and suicidal behavior.*

We'll look at shame a little later, but for now we'll focus on the "thoughts of suicide and suicidal behavior." This is a major area of concern because some statistics state that **8-10 percent of all people with BPD commit suicide.**

That's a terribly high percentage as it is, but the number could actually be much higher because it only includes people who were diagnosed with BPD. Many high-functioning BPs are never diagnosed and therefore suicides within that group are not counted as BPD-related.

Does the BP truly want to die or are they crying out for help? In my situation, it was definitely both.

Suicide is the decisive solution to mood swings and depression. A BP would never again have to experience the desperate fear of being left alone to face their own lack of self. In one blazing moment of feeling alive, all their problems are removed.

Attempted suicide is also an excellent method to attract attention. No matter how many arguments a marriage might face, when a BP tries to end it all, the spouse will rush to offer compassion and support. It's a game changer to be sure. Or at least it should be.

Lyssa's first of four suicidal events (there were likely more I don't know about) was before we'd been married a year, and I did a very poor job of taking it seriously at the time.

In an argument I felt was over nothing, she leapt to an extreme response. She soon locked herself in the bathroom and announced she had taken a handful of pills because she didn't want to live anymore.

Lyssa was having some thyroid problems and had been taking medication for only a week, so she still had a large supply of capsules, and that's what she "overdosed" on.

I had never heard of suicide by thyroid medication but didn't want to take any chances. I looked it up on the internet and determined there was no danger. I waited for her to come out of the bathroom on her own and monitored her the rest of the evening to make sure she was okay.

Was this a legitimate attempt to kill herself? Probably not. The pills she took simply weren't a mortal threat. But this is where I dropped the ball.

I didn't treat her threat of suicide as a serious problem. Instead, I was so relieved that she hadn't tried something more effective that I overlooked the underlying problem. She was symbolically screaming for me to see the desperate place she found herself, and I just wasn't prepared to hear her.

I didn't want to confront that I had a wife disturbed enough to take her own life, so I told myself she hadn't really done it. If it didn't count as a *real* suicide attempt, I didn't have to take any special action. Yup, that was my logic.

The second suicidal event was referred to earlier when, in the midst of a rage, she yelled out, "The only reason I'm not killing myself right now is the thought of what it would do to my little sister."

The amount of pain someone must feel to commit suicide terrifies me. I didn't want to think I could have anything to do with causing such anguish. Therefore, I disconnected from the moment.

She had used the word suicide, but she hadn't actually committed a physical act. That means she didn't really mean it, right? It was just a nasty attempt to make me give in to whatever ridiculous demands she was making. "I'll show her," I thought. "Instead of racing to give her comfort, I'll just sit here and act completely unmoved by her plea."

She was begging for help. But once again, I was unable to grasp the severity of the moment. I had become numb to her drama and threats, and refused to give an inch to any of her demands.

In her angry fits, she would often yell out extreme comments like, "This is a nightmare," "I'll never forgive you for this," or "This is the worst thing that's ever happened to me." I had conditioned myself to not respond when she used these demonstratives, and her talk of suicide got lumped in with the rest.

The third suicidal event came quite a bit later during our 4th year of marriage.

I'll talk about what led up to it later in the "Anger" chapter, but in my attempt to leave during one of her rages, she screamed at me in a public setting that if I left, she would kill herself that very minute.

Unlike the previous threats, I actually considered this one believable. Her tone of desperation was at an all-new level. It stopped me in my tracks, and I didn't leave. That time, we sought help.

Therapist #5

Rather than seek counseling directly concerning her talk of suicide, Lyssa and I decided to try marriage counseling again. She had mentioned the topic to an acquaintance she deeply trusted and he said, "I know a guy. He saved my marriage."

So, we were soon seated in the office of Dr. Heath surrounded by Persian rugs, indoor water features, soothing harp music, and the scent of sage. I immediately liked him and his white-haired ponytail for being an unapologetic New Age stereotype.

Lyssa informed him that our previous counselors had all been blacklisted because of their uninformed assumptions of borderline personality disorder.

He nodded in understanding and started off by walking us through some basic communication techniques with an emphasis on listening without judgement.

He asked me what I had hoped to get out of being married and I said, "I love the idea of being married, but I no longer believe that *this* marriage will survive without drastic changes."

My answer was a bit of a dodge. Rather than trash our marriage, I trashed the current *status* of our marriage.

My honesty during our counseling sessions began an ugly weekly cycle. On our drive home, Lyssa would get angry and cry about the awful things I said, and we'd have an immense argument *about* marriage counseling. As if we didn't already have enough fuel to ignite.

It was that environment that led to Lyssa's fourth suicidal event.

At one of our therapy meetings, we needed to take separate cars, but that didn't stop Lyssa from her post-session anxiety attack. She raged at me in the parking lot about how insensitive I was and that if she was so horrible, I should just leave her and get it over with.

Lyssa became louder and utterly inconsolable. I refused to be pulled into her usual baiting techniques and began getting in my car to leave. She screamed at me that she would finally kill herself if I didn't stay and somehow make it all better.

Instead, I walked back to Dr. Heath's office and let his staff know what was happening outside. I explained that I would be leaving and they agreed she could come inside to calm down.

What Dr. Heath did from that point was brilliant. He knew that if BPD was mentioned, she would shut him out. But he found another point of entry to crack open the door—through the topic of *shame*. From the first time he brought it up, she was willing to listen.

Shame and Borderline Personality Disorder
In *Stop Walking on Eggshells*, the authors say:

> In their typical all-or-nothing way, people with BPD may either become consumed by their shame or deny to themselves and others that it even exists.

You and I might experience shame for some of our past actions: those nagging moments where we cringe over an act we wish could be erased from our memory. But then, the moment passes, and we continue on with the day. Not so for the BP.

Many BPs suffer from a pervasive level of shame that leaves them helpless to their feelings. They swirl in a state of worthlessness, isolation, and failure.

A BP in this condition not only fights to hide their shame from others, but also from themselves. Admitting their shame only exacerbates their guilt and misery, so, like criminals and politicians, they deny, deny, deny.

Oddly, the external symptoms of such toxic shame can be polar extremes. Some BPs turn to rage as a means to deny their shame. Other choose to become excessive people-pleasers or caretakers.

In my case with Lyssa, I saw both reactions, often within short spans of time. She could just as easily yell about not giving a damn what I thought to being deeply sullen if I didn't show my approval.

For the non-BP, getting sucked into the gravity of the BP's shame-state is a wild ride of unpredictability. In my frustration from seeing Lyssa swing across the spectrum, I would often say things like, "I wish you would just pick a side already!" And no, that never helped.

Fortunately, Dr. Heath had a more experienced approach to deal with these issues. He expertly tapped into Lyssa's past, specifically as connected to her father. He provided some excellent literature on shame and asked us both to read it.

Not unlike our previous attempts with therapists, it didn't take long for most of his attention to be focused on her. I seldom spoke at all after her recent threat of suicide. I'm sure she picked up on what he was doing, but the topic of shame held her attention.

For the first time that I had ever seen, Lyssa was showing a willingness to address an issue in therapy that was about her, and not strictly me or us. Was this the beginning of a healing path?

What I Wish I Had Done

From the very first instance of suicidal behavior, I should have reached out for help. Or at the very least, I should have expressed to Lyssa in a calm moment that any future mention of suicide would result in an emergency 911 call. No exceptions.

To reiterate, at least 8-10 percent of all BPs commit suicide, probably more if those who remain undiagnosed are included. I'm fortunate I didn't lose Lyssa in those days. One rash act and there would have been no do-overs. Her crushing fears of non-existence would have come true.

According to the National Institute of Mental Health, the spouse of a BP should:

> *Take seriously any comments about suicide or wishing to die. Even if you do not believe your family member or friend will attempt suicide, the person is clearly in distress and can benefit from your help in finding treatment.*

Help can be found by calling the National Suicide Prevention Lifeline toll-free at 1–800–273–TALK (8255), 24 hours a day, 7 days a week. The deaf and hard of hearing can contact the lifeline via TTY at 1–800–799–4889. All calls are free and confidential.

To learn how anger is another serious symptom of BPD, keep reading.

CHAPTER 9: ANGER

BPDs may display inappropriate, intense anger or
problems controlling anger

Obviously, by now you've read numerous examples of BP anger. If you're married to a BP, you are quite familiar with the concept of seemingly unpredictable and inconsolable rage. It is an awesome spectacle to behold.

This symptom seems to outweigh all the others as far as its effect on the non-BP, but the *DSM-5* addresses it in a short statement:

> *Persistent or frequent angry feelings; anger or irritability in response to minor slights and insults.*

"Irritability" hardly seems an adequate description when you're ducking dishes being thrown at you. The *DSM-IV* was still brief but assigns a little more bite:

> *Inappropriate, intense anger or difficulty controlling anger (e.g., frequent displays of temper, constant anger, recurrent physical fights).*

Merri Lisa Johnson, in her memoir *Girl in Need of a Tourniquet*, brilliantly offers this vivid description of BPD anger:

> *Our rage is perverse. Like a strange child, the rage walks backwards. Sarcasm takes scattered steps in a zigzag towards the beloved...High-pitched shrieks followed by the sound of air entering a slit throat is borderline for PLEASE STAY.*

Society has attempted to limit when it seems appropriate to express anger. Examples include:

--athletes in competitive sports
--someone cuts you off in traffic
--someone threaten you or your family
--your boss berates you unfairly
--Ross and Rachel *almost* get back together but then don't

Here, on the other hand, is a brief list of events that sparked off-the-hook anger in Lyssa. I'm talking full-on, hours-long rage fests:

--I won at Scrabble when the app didn't score us correctly
--I asked a stranger for directions
--I high-fived someone
--I applauded at a music performance
--I played music while she got ready for us to go out
--I didn't look away from Victoria's Secret commercial on TV
--I looked away from a Victoria's Secret commercial on TV in a way that made fun of the fact that she insisted I look away

I can infuse a little humor about it now, but it was no joke when it happened. Here's a journal entry as an example:

Year 4, March:

Today I came home and found a large pile of crushed and broken CDs in the middle of the living room floor.

Last week Lyssa confronted me about my CD collection: "Why do you have more women artists than men?" Confused, I asked why I shouldn't. She implied that I was being sexist and just falling for the marketing of women's sexuality. I pointed out that the female artists I liked were not really in the "pop" realm she was referring to, but rather true musicians, songwriters, and producers: Joni Mitchell, Kate Bush, Bjork, etc. I also pointed out that if you include CDs from bands, I had way more from men singers. She said, "that didn't count," with no explanation. How convenient for her.

This began a dreadful argument in which she insisted that I have to listen to more male music than female. How can a person realistically even keep score of such a crazy notion? But she didn't care about logic. She was just acting nuts and I told her so.

So, there on the floor was her response. She had shattered over a dozen CDs from female solo artists and left them as a warning that calling her "nuts" was not a good idea.

Have you ever tried to shatter a CD? It's a seriously violent act. And she committed it about 15 times.

Even though this event took place several years into our marriage, I suspect she had been counting my CDs by gender since we started dating.

During our first summer together, she randomly gifted me several Josh Groban CDs. I listened to each one and then put them on the shelf with the rest of my collection.

A short time later she asked in a hurt tone, "Why don't you listen more to Josh Groban? Don't you appreciate my gift?" Even then, she was trying to navigate me away from the female artists that threatened her. This was obviously the seed of what would become a field of poison ivy.

Here's another example of BP anger from my journal:

Year 4, September:

Today I had to have Lyssa escorted from my workplace. She started an argument this morning because I refused to stop reading an article in the paper about a local strip club that recently opened. I said, "You know, with all the serious problems in the world, I wish we could argue about something that actually matters sometime." She began fuming and insisted I apologize, but I had to leave for work and said we could talk about it later.

Without notice, she showed up at my office and attempted to keep the argument going. I refused to engage with her and she swept her arm across a shelf, knocking all the contents to the floor. I called security to report I had a violent person in my office. As they removed her, she called me a coward who "couldn't even stand up to a girl."

This was from the same person who accused me of abuse if I *did* stand up to her. But as a BP, her past doesn't factor in as a consequence to current actions.

On the occasions I said something like, "I'm going to change the way I do things because of your previous behavior," she would look at me with zero comprehension. It's like she thought I must have been talking about someone else.

Every Four Days

During the heights of Lyssa's most intensely regular anger episodes (which ironically was while I attended court-mandated anger management classes), I noticed a pattern.

After one of Lyssa's rages, I found that I could put a mark four days later on the calendar and know that's when Lyssa would have her next melt down.

This cycle became horrifically predictable and lasted for months. It got to the point where I scheduled life events around those upcoming dates. Someone would invite us to a gathering in the next week and I'd say, "Sorry, I know we'll be busy that night." And sure enough, we were.

Come day four, I would be wound up tight trying to avoid saying anything to wake the dragon. But even saying nothing would bring down the rain. The Crazy in her simply had to come out—the reason why didn't matter—it was going to happen.

Rules Police

Most of the fits of anger I experienced with Lyssa were directed at me. But there was one group of people she would get mad at, even if they were complete strangers: rule breakers.

Lyssa assigned herself the role of "Rules Police" when she was in the public and took this position very seriously. There were multiple occasions where she was perfectly willing to put herself (or me) in danger simply to enforce the rules as she saw them.

Here's a relevant example from my journal:

Year 5, December:

We celebrated our 5th anniversary at Disneyland during a trip to California. The day was argument free and we had a nice time except for a tense exchange between us and another couple.

We arrived early at a parade-watching point in order to claim some premium viewing space. As the minutes ticked off, more people arrived and began crowding in on our area. One couple got particularly close, but it wasn't unreasonable considering there were thousands of people jockeying for spots.

Lyssa challenged the interlopers by spreading her feet apart, planting herself aggressively in front of them, and proclaiming loudly, "We got here first and no one is allowed to come along at the last minute to push us out!"

The couple in front of us were some very tough looking characters—right out of central casting for Latino gang members. The woman (with an easy 50 pounds over Lyssa) responded with, "Maybe you'd like to move me little girl." Lyssa shot right back and they were getting in each other's faces at full volume.

The guy and I shared a hapless shrug and eye-roll combo that said, "Oh man, here we go again!" We both knew that if they started throwing down, we'd get dragged into it to "protect our women" and it would be a huge mess.

Fortunately, some people next to us—probably freaked out by the arguing girls—vacated their spot, opening up some breathing room for the four of us. A fist fight at the happiest place on earth was narrowly avoided.

Lyssa also felt particularly aggressive about enforcing rules while she was driving. She would go to extreme measures to "teach them a lesson" if she thought anyone else was not following the traffic laws.

There was a double-turning-lane intersection near our home that wasn't marked well and sometimes drivers from the left lane would veer into the right without realizing the mistake. Not so when Lyssa was behind the wheel.

She would hold her right-lane position even if she saw a car coming straight towards her, calling out, "Someone has to show them they're wrong!" Her car was sideswiped twice while being the boss of that intersection.

She pulled the same kind of maneuver on a freeway onramp that resulted in an act of road rage against us. With Lyssa refusing to drive faster than the posted (and rather slow) speed limit as two lanes funneled together, a driver in the merging lane swerved and braked hard to avoid hitting us.

Lyssa made no attempt to go faster or make room because, "they shouldn't be speeding." As the other driver recovered and pushed their way through by using the emergency lane, they shot something hard at Lyssa's window, leaving a crack. Their window rolled up before I could see if it was a pellet gun or sling shot.

These were just two traffic scenarios I was involved in. Over the years, I found an increasing number of scratches, dents, and cracks on Lyssa's car that she had no explanation for. Who knows how many times she got into altercations when I wasn't present?

Our Last Fight

During our 4th year of marriage, Lyssa got an incredible offer. She was accepted for graduate studies in her chosen field at one of the premiere universities in the country, if not the world. She would be given free tuition and a small stipend for work-study within the department. We would only need to cover living expenses.

There was a downside. The location of the school was an 8-hour drive from the job I needed to keep in order to pay for two households. This was a dream opportunity for Lyssa, so I could hardly offer opposition. We decided to make the sacrifice of living apart while she completed her master's degree.

During that first year, the effects on our marriage were double-edged. While we were apart, we didn't argue much and regained an appreciation for each other. We took notice of the little things that didn't get done when the other person wasn't around. That's good for a relationship, and it was easy to say, "I miss you."

However, while we were together for weekend and holiday visits, we seemed to make up for lost time by compressing more arguments than ever into the limited period we had.

This only made me *more* upset because I felt she was ruining our rare together-time for completely unworthy reasons. Of course, me accusing her of getting mad "over nothing" only spun her into further rage and insisting that I apologize.

The worst example of this cycle occurred during a 3-day weekend when I drove to her city. Traffic was bad so the trip took over nine hours and I arrived tired and frazzled.

I had only just set my bags down when Lyssa attacked me for some imaginary slight that I had done. I had warned her ahead of time that we needed to be kind to each other during our visit or there would be consequences.

Without saying much of anything, I simply picked up my bag and walked towards the door. I wasn't going to drive all the way back home, but I could at least make it to a cheap, freeway hotel and finish the trip in the morning.

Lyssa went into full-panic mode and raced to block the door. Instead of calming down to keep me from leaving, she got more aggressive and doubled down on her verbal attack. I was a "thoughtless, insensitive, cowardly, unloving, mean-spirited, evil husband" who didn't deserve a wife who loved me like she did.

She even tried a new trick—comparing me to a former professor of mine whose wife had divorced him late in life, leaving him lonely and desperate. She sniped, "I'll dump you and you'll end up just like Dr. Juarez!" I'd had enough of the abuse and got past her to open the door.

As I firmly walked down the apartment building hallway, Lyssa followed me and screamed, "PLEASE DON'T LEAVE!" I kept moving without looking back.

Then, in a last attempt to manipulate me, "IF YOU DON'T COME BACK, I'LL KILL MYSELF RIGHT THIS MINUTE!"

Her tone was believable. The amount of pain in her tear-stained face was palpable. So much suffering. So much confusion. I came back.

In the midst of my self-loathing for giving in to her suicidal threats, I sternly announced that I would stay the weekend as we planned, but that I wouldn't talk or engage with her in any way.

From my perspective, she had ruined any chance for us to enjoy ourselves, and I was staying *only* because of her threat and nothing else. I parked on the sofa where I would silently reside for the next three days before finally leaving.

Within 30 minutes after I came back in, she asked if we could make love.

That is what it's like to be married to a Borderline.

CHAPTER 10: DISSOCIATION

*BPDs may display feelings of dissociation, such as
feeling cut off from oneself, observing oneself from
outside one's body, or feelings of unreality*

Of all the BPD symptoms, this is the one I find the most "out there." The concept of dissociation is very difficult for a non-BP to grasp. It is for me anyway, and I still struggle with it.

First, let's see what the experts say. The *DSM-IV* offers this soundbite:

> *Transient, stress-related paranoid ideation or severe dissociative symptoms.*

Not much help there, right? We need more.

DSM-5 provides additional direction by telling us to look for impairment in self functioning, including:

> *Markedly impoverished, poorly developed, or unstable self-image, often associated with excessive self-criticism; chronic feelings of emptiness; dissociative states under stress.*

That's more helpful. At least now we see that "dissociative states" are connected to the issue of unstable self-image. By now, you've learned in this book that sense of self is one of the most difficult and pervasive symptoms a BP faces. If that symptom is alleviated, many of the others are likely to diminish.

Mild forms of dissociation are common to most of us. Maybe you're reading this book and realize a couple pages have gone by without you having any memory of the words. Or perhaps you've driven to and from work so many times that you sometimes arrive at the other end with little knowledge of what the trip was like.

For the BP, dissociation occurs at a more extreme level, especially if the related event is painful or stressful. It's even possible that you and your wife will remember the same situation in vastly different terms due to her dissociation.

I recall several instances of me disputing Lyssa in a flurry, "I was there too, and you don't get to just rewrite our history like that."

From my journal:

Year 1, October:
We had a terrible argument last night. Furniture was knocked over. Dishes broken. She actually smashed a 3-foot hole in the drywall near the kitchen. Almost as if waking up from a hangover like a couple of drunks, this morning we cleaned up the tatters and began repairing the damage in silence. Like misbehaving visitors had done it and we were left to tidy up.

The visible proof of her rage would be denied or merely transferred to me. "I wouldn't have done that if you had given me comfort like I asked for." The Crazy does not like looking in a mirror.

After I noticed several of my precious pre-marital keepsakes had disappeared, I confronted Lyssa. She denied any responsibility, but I held firm and insisted her acts of thievery were completely unacceptable. I essentially went on strike and refused any interaction with her until my possessions were returned.

After a couple days, she came into the house with a large sack of booty. She had stolen far more than I was aware of. While handing me the evidence of her crimes, she insinuated she wasn't sure how she came across it. She wanted me to believe that the bag had simply "shown up" and that I should reward her for its return.

The truth was unpleasant, so dissociation rescued her from the responsibility.

She's not complaining, so I guess everything's fine

After the stunning display of suicidal threats, traumatic public outburst, and complete emotional upheaval Lyssa and I had faced, I was mortified to imagine what could come next.

How would the Crazy top those performances? Was there any upper limit to the shear lunacy to be faced in the future? I prepared myself for actions without any rational boundaries or moral grounding.

Indeed, something quite insidious occurred that was beyond all preconception or expectation...

...nothing.

Zippo. Nada.

No more fights. No more accusations. No more broken or stolen possessions. No more verbal abuse. Just...nothing.

I loved it! And I definitely didn't want to screw it up by asking her about the change. The less said, the less chance I might poke the dragon.

We were now past our 5-year anniversary and I thought, "If what we've gone through couldn't take us down, *nothing* will!" Only solid, lasting marriages make it beyond five years, right?

The trade-off I saw to Lyssa's lack of BPD symptoms was an equal lack of feeling of any sort. I was thrilled that she stopped the anger bombs and crying jags, but she also seldom laughed or expressed enthusiasm. We kind of just mutedly co-existed in the same space.

I intellectually understood that her blunt affect was the marker of an unhealthy mind, but I just couldn't pass up the opportunity to enjoy some calm in our lives. "I'll bring it up eventually, but not today..." Or the next.

Her indifference seeped into our sex life as well, already sporadic because of living in two distant cities. She dryly offered, "You'll have to initiate having sex. Those thoughts just aren't coming to me these days."

Fine by me. One less thing to fight about.

Looking back on it, after that last big fight, she probably started taking anti-depressants but didn't want to admit it to me, and I didn't want to know so long as the raging stopped.

A Grand Gesture

A couple months short of our sixth anniversary, I noticed some unwarranted swelling in my left leg. Over the phone, Lyssa said, "Rob, please get to the doctor." Fortunately, I listened to her.

Shortly after having my general practitioner examine me, I was caught up in a blur of tests and a look of obvious concern by the medical staff buzzing around me.

Diagnosis: chronic deep vein thrombosis—a large blood clot running from my left ankle all the way up to my crotch. One of the technicians pressed an amplified stethoscope to my leg and asked, "You notice the silence?" I nodded. "Yeah, that's not good," he added. "People have strokes and die from these things all the time." I was unnerved, to say the least.

The immediate medical response was to keep me immobilized on a hospital bed for four nights, including one night in the intensive care unit. This was serious stuff.

In a grand gesture of loving concern, Lyssa totally stepped up. She drove the eight hours to be with me by that first night in the hospital. Sleeping on a small mat in a window alcove, she never left my side.

When I was having a medium-sized breakdown from fatigue and fear of needles, her wife-bear instincts totally kicked in. She doggedly pursued the staff until I was given the care my situation needed. In a word, she was amazing, and I will never forget it.

A couple months later, we traveled to my home state for our anniversary and visited with friends and family. Everyone had a nice time, and unlike the complete catastrophe of a previous visit, nothing went wrong. It actually felt odd. I enjoyed the pleasantness, but was somewhat on edge thinking it might be an elaborate trap.

She was allowing us a basically calm marriage — and it was kind of freaking me out.

The Writing on the Wall

Not long after our sixth anniversary, I drove through four states to visit Lyssa for several days while she house-sat for one of her professors. She said there was news to share.

Lyssa was so well-liked in her master's program that she was invited to stay and earn a doctorate degree under full scholarship. I was happy for her. She had worked hard and deserved the platitudes.

Our original plan was for her to finish a master's and then we would reunite our lives to the same address and put into motion getting pregnant. But now, she was talking about another advanced degree that could easily take an additional three years to complete.

I congratulated her on the amazing opportunity and said I would totally support her decision to pursue a doctorate. Afterall, I didn't want to be "that guy" who says, "Give up your dreams and start having babies."

I told her, "Go for it!" She said, "I will."

Our reaction was all a lie of course, but neither of us was ready to confront it. The truth was, she didn't want to come back home and start a family. And I liked the decision to keep us living apart being her fault instead of mine.

Later that night, it occurred to me we hadn't had sex for months. I felt awkward about not making the effort. If we have sex, there must not be anything wrong with our marriage, right?

While I was on top of her, she looked away and covered her eyes with the back of her hand. Her revulsion was undeniable. I had initiated intimacy without desire, and she countered by agreeing to the same.

I've heard men joke that there's no such thing as bad sex. Oh contraire, mon frère! I've experienced it firsthand and don't ever want to know that feeling again.

While getting dressed afterwards, she sincerely asked, "Was that nice?" I managed to nod in approval and gave her a smile, which she returned. I'm pretty sure she had dissociated entirely with what we had just experienced. At that moment, I envied her.

There was nothing left between us. The BPD had completely vanquished all opposition to its domination. I had blundered my way for over six years trying to negotiate, tolerate, accommodate, medicate, and even subjugate. I had failed.

The Crazy had won.

CHAPTER 11: OTHER SYMPTOMS

Besides the chapter titles and pervasive shame that we discussed earlier, there are a handful of other behaviors also considered to be traits of BPD. None of them will get an entire chapter of their own here, but that doesn't mean they aren't to be taken seriously.

While these traits may only receive a brief mention in the *DSM* editions, researchers consider them common enough to be discussed in the lexicon of BPD behavior.

Risk Taking

BPs can be the ultimate members of the YOLO (you only live once) crowd. With an unstable or practically non-existent sense of self, a BP might pursue any number of dangerous activities in order to feel alive. These are actions purely for the thrill, rather than self-harm.

Prime examples include: one-night stands, group sex, extreme sports, starting fights in public, goading others to fight, gambling money they can't afford to lose, and aggressive driving.

Emptiness

The emptiness a BP feels is far more profound than what you and I experience. While we can hopefully convince ourselves that our feelings of emptiness are temporary, and therefore manageable, the BP considers them hopeless and infinite.

I could spot feelings of emptiness in Lyssa by her use of demonstratives. Like a toddler convinced the world is ending because of being told "no," a BP will shout, "I'll NEVER forgive you," and "You ALWAYS leave when I need you the most."

Mistrust

As you can imagine, if your wife is constantly terrified you will abandon her, she may not be able trust you. Trying to tell a BP that you love them is like quenching their thirst with an eyedropper. The moment you give them a drop, they immediately crave more. When you balk at delivering an endless supply, they mistrust your motives and attack you.

Like I mentioned earlier, the moment you scratch an item off your list of "Things My Wife Gets Upset About," she's added three more. And given enough time, any problem you think was handled in the past will come roaring back bigger and meaner for being ignored.

Interpersonal Sensitivity

Many BPs have the ability to quickly assess personality keystones in others and make use of the information to get what they need. This is extremely helpful in the workplace and allows BPs to succeed and be well liked.

I noticed this about Lyssa early on. She picked up on my signals, whether I knew I was sending them or not, and "magically" became increasingly attractive to me. Because she lacked a strong sense of self, she looked to me for ideas and embraced them for her own.

Control Issues

Often feeling helpless and without self-identity, a BP might overcompensate by aggressively trying to control people and situations around them. Following in the symptom of "extremes," the BP will see their world as either right or wrong. Everything is either in its place (on time, on budget, picture perfect, etc.), or it is wrong. No grey area.

I remember many frustrating occasions when Lyssa would accuse me of trying to control her reactions at the very moment her reactions were trying to control me. It was a vicious cycle. We would soon act like children saying silly things like, "No I'm not. *You* are!"

Situational Competence

This symptom is very common among the high-functioning BPs I described early in the book. While their personal relationships are a cesspool of disaster, the BP may be exceedingly successful in other areas. This is likely the case at school, work, athletics, or a serious hobby.

In this regard, the BP is taking control issues and focusing them on being productive. If you want a project done on time and near perfect, put a Borderline on the job.

Lyssa was brilliant as an artist. She would dedicate 6-8 hours a day to perfecting her craft and think nothing of it. This was easily the most impressive positive characteristic I saw in her personality.

Impaired self-direction

Conversely, a BP may enter phases where their life shatters and nothing gets accomplished. They ask, "How can I think about finding a job when I'm not even sure I exist?" The feelings of emptiness and despair take over and can't be overridden.

Eventually, the mood swings the other direction and a phase of positive-minded productivity begins again.

At our worst point, I learned that Lyssa would become severely impaired about every four days. Her goals for life would simply break like fragile glass against the unstoppable force of her depression.

In her fear, she would find a fault in anything I did and attack. It was never about me, but it sure felt like it at the time.

No Object Constancy

Earlier, I talked about how babies can't conceive of a thing's existence if it is not within their range of senses. When they don't hear, see, taste, smell, or feel mom, she's no longer in the realm of perception.

As adults, we have developed the skills to handle the absence of someone we care about. We miss them dearly, but understand that someday, the feeling will recede. Not so the BP.

To them, they still cling to their infant-like belief that an object is not constant. If they can't keep it in the room, it's never coming back. Imagine how terrifying life is for your wife when you step out the door during an angry moment.

When Lyssa and I would argue and I would leave or refuse to interact with her, I would often find her laying on the floor surrounded by letters and cards I had written her. If she couldn't have me, at least she could try to confirm my existence (and therefore hers) with personal items I had given her.

The image of seeing her that way still breaks my heart all these years later. I just didn't know.

Narcissistic Demands

I have read that about 25% of BPs also have narcissistic personality disorder. The narcissist is known for constantly drawing attention back to themselves, especially in public.

Like a child throwing a tantrum, a BP will act out in movie theaters, stores, amusement parks, and church. She will want others to see and verify that you aren't being a good husband who supports his wife's needs.

Lyssa's chosen locations for narcissistic episodes were amusement parks and Walmart. The large crowds and abundance of BPD triggers made for a volatile cocktail of emotions.

Boundaries

Try setting a personal boundary with a BP and you will rapidly learn how much they don't like such things. Sentences that include "but" are a common trigger. "I love you, but…" "I know you'd like me to stay, but…" "This may feel acceptable to you, but…" All of these statements set boundaries. They draw lines that society says will activate consequences if you cross them.

In the all-or-nothing, right-or-wrong world of the BP, boundaries are meant to be blasted asunder in a fiery rage.

You'll need to learn how to set firm boundaries if your wife has BPD, and be prepared to keep mending your scorched and splintered road block a thousand times.

♦ ♦ ♦

My Wife Asks Me to Ask Her to Ask for a Divorce
The months following our sixth anniversary saw a continuation of our new-found détente. Lyssa remained detached from her emotions and I remained suspicious that it couldn't last.

For the first time in our marriage, we weren't fighting. It felt wonderful. My perspective was that things were clearly not great between us, but at least we were in a position to start working on the problems. We wouldn't be continuously sidetracked by the rage du jour.

As for me, I found myself much more willing to make compromises when I didn't feel under attack. Lyssa expressed a few things she wished were different in our relationship and I think I stunned her by agreeing without dissention. It was almost as if she had counted on me to disagree and was disappointed I hadn't.

As we approached her spring break, she added some heat to what I suspected were attempts to goad me.

As we discussed me visiting her for the week she was out of school, she said, "It looks like my sister Caroline will be visiting with us at the same time. I hope you don't mind."

I did mind. We hadn't seen each other in a couple of months and she seemed all too willing to diminish our alone-time by adding a family member. But, in the spirit of our recent placidity, I said, "Sure, it will be nice to see her." After a couple seconds of silence, Lyssa said, "Oh? Okay."

A few days later, she called to say, "Caroline and I have made plans for the three of us to visit with our grandparents during spring break. I hope that's okay with you."

It wasn't. Her grandparents lived four hours further than the eight hours I was already driving to get to Lyssa's apartment. This would eat away most of another day from our already limited time together.

I could tell I was being played. Lyssa simply didn't want to see me but couldn't come right out and say it. She was throwing down obstacles, hoping I would be the one to bail out.

It worked. I said, "You know, I'm not interested in spending so much time in a car to be with family when it should be the two of us alone trying to keep a marriage going. I'm going to take a pass on this one." She jumped on the opening I provided. "Well, I wish you'd come, but I understand."

For the first time, I had flat out refused to give her something she asked for, and instead of anger she showed no disappointment whatsoever. Her lack of response was a direct-hit cannon shot. Something big was going on.

As spring break drew closer, she presented a litany of small annoyances: she might not have much time to see me in the summer; she would be needing more money; her car needed maintenance;

talking on the phone every night was distracting her from schoolwork; etc.

This was the kind of day-to-day marriage stuff I thrived on. No arguments, just boring problems that could be handled with some basic communication and planning. I generally responded with, "Sure. We'll work it out."

My willingness to bend in the face of continued mild blustering finally drew her out.

She began telling me how depressed she was about our marriage and that she wasn't being the kind of wife I probably needed. "I mean, I'm never around for you anymore. What's the point? People don't need to stay married in these kinds of situations. Maybe it's better if they try another path."

She just couldn't pull the trigger. My wife was asking me to ask her to ask for a divorce.

"Lyssa," I said, "I believe the word you're getting around to is 'divorce.'" To which she calmly replied, "I guess so."

With a throwback to her seeing our relationship through the eyes of a forever-adolescent BP, she enthusiastically added, "And if we don't like it, we can just get married again later!"

Yeah, that never happened.

Lyssa and I did very little talking about the "why" as soon as the D-word had been used out loud. We basically moved right into "how" and "when."

We also never talked about the fact that I had aggressively sought a divorce several years earlier, but she implored me to not leave. So much pain and wasted time that could have been avoided.

Now that divorce was *her* proposition, she was slightly annoyed at me for jumping into the process so quickly, but we didn't fight about it. Once the decision had been made, I offered no resistance.

Being married to Lyssa was something I had resigned myself to, but if she wanted out, I knew it was only going to make my life easier. Sooner the better.

There was talk of her coming to our home to collect what she wanted from our belongings, but that didn't happen. She didn't want anything to do with returning to the scene of the crimes.

There was nothing left in our marriage for her to consume. The well was dry. Something must have snapped in her mind just after the last suicidal threat when I agreed to stay with her for three days but refused to interact with her or even acknowledge her presence.

Since that day, there was a clear change in her. That was her line in the sand that I had crossed over.

I suspect she thought, "If I can't even convince him to love me by threatening to kill myself, he's really no good to me." The Crazy knew there was no point in hanging around: "Surely, there must be someone else out there ready to play the game."

Men beware. Those delicious homemade cookies ain't free.

CHAPTER 12: WHAT CAME NEXT?

Okay, we've finished our discussion of BPD symptoms and how I experienced them with my wife. I have to ask; how often did you see yourself in these pages? Did it make you cringe? Laugh? Shake your head?

After all of my sometimes-difficult revelations, perhaps you're wondering how it all worked out for the main players. Did we reconcile? Submit ourselves to intense therapy? Find true love? Become friends? Not learn from our mistakes and repeat the process all over again?

I'll tell you what I can.

Robert Page

I spent the first few months after my divorce in a complete fog and quite miserable.

I was surprised that I didn't find myself missing Lyssa at all. I missed the act of being married, but not my actual wife. We were so toxic for each other that I completely concurred divorce was the best outcome. Once the decision was made, I moved quickly to get it over with and move on.

Because her school residence was in a more progressive state than our home, we were able to file a no-fault divorce there that didn't require financial disclosures or lawyers. I wrote a check to her for half the equity in the house, divided up possessions and the meager savings account, and that was about it. Don't get me wrong, the divorce process totally sucks, but compared to other examples I've seen, our "splitting the sheets" was fast-tracked and comparably smooth.

We met at the courthouse to go over the final documents with a judge. Lyssa and I chatted comfortably while we waited for our appointment. We even managed to make a couple jokes. I don't remember if we hugged goodbye...but we weren't angry with each other.

That was the last time I ever saw her.

It should be noted that during this timeframe I still didn't blame BPD for all our problems (most, but not all). I still pondered if it was just the two of us "not getting along" well enough to want to stay together. It was only in the following years that I finally admitted what the root cause was and educate myself.

At the time of our divorce I felt like an utter failure as a man and husband. I had been unable to save my damsel in distress. No shining hero was I. And this belief sent me spiraling into depression.

No sleep. No appetite. No motivation. I watched old movies like *Casablanca* dozens of times to fill the void. My work life became a mindless drudgery. I was a failure, and failures aren't allowed to be in a good mood. If I couldn't be a success at marriage, then I would damn well be successful at failing! I pretty much nailed it for a while.

But I slowly came around. A co-worker started hitting on me once she noticed I wasn't wearing my wedding ring. The weight I had lost due to not eating actually motivated me to get healthy and stay trim. I pulled the classic mid-life crisis maneuver and bought a 2-seater sports car. I found a couple other single guys to hang out with. One had even dated a BP and we bonded over the shared experience.

Yup, my pre-marriage mojo was coming back.

Before the year was out, I had lost 40 pounds, embraced minimalism, gotten rid of almost everything that didn't fit in the impractically small (but fast) car, sold the house Lyssa and I had lived in, quit my job, and drove west into the sunset towards my native home. Led Zeppelin cranked up while rolling across Route 66 was the best therapy I could have given myself.

From that point on, my life's trajectory shot up like a rocket. I lived on a sailboat, made love to beautiful women, started writing books I truly believed in, reconnected with friends I had been cut off from (they graciously accepted me back), and found a new career that most people would consider "living the dream." None of which would have happened if I had stayed with Lyssa.

But easily the best thing that has come my way is a new wife, Irene. She was a childhood sweetheart who I had not seen for several decades, and we are now crazy-happy in love. Everything I had ever imagined marriage could be is coming true. It turns out I'm a mighty good husband when given a fair shot.

I have to admit, I spent the first year of our relationship waiting for the Crazy to show up. Even after our wedding I was looking for signs. Nope. They never appeared. We're just normal, content people dealing with both the good times and disagreements like grownups.

Irene has no idea how many times a day I do or say things that were considered dangerous if not outright forbidden in the 1.0 marriage.

A small version of the list includes: referring to ex-girlfriends, watching video/TV with sexual content, asking a woman on the street for directions, looking at a lifestyle magazine, reading the news, walking through a mall, listening to random music, laughing at a joke, talking about my past, saying goodnight without a scripted checklist, seeing friends without her, and just sitting around doing a bunch of nothing.

Irene might not see it as a compliment, but anyone ever married to a BP will understand what I mean by this next statement:

Oh! how I love being in a perfectly boring relationship.

Lyssa

It's now been many years since I've had any contact with my former wife. It's a blessing we never had children because it's clear that we didn't have a need to stay in touch on our own. Preparing for this book, I searched for her name on the internet, but she continues to maintain a very small digital footprint and there isn't much to find. I discovered no evidence that she finished her doctorate degree.

She moved in with a man shortly after our divorce, but I don't know if they ever married or had children. Unless she immediately entered into therapy (extremely doubtful), I cannot conceive of her maintaining a relationship longer than ours (about 7 years total). I just don't see her finding a man more patient than I was. But maybe that's just my vanity. Anything's possible, and a woman as intelligent as her might have found a way.

This will sound awful, but I have to say it: unless she completed years of therapy for her BPD, I hope she never had children. The psychic damage she would inflict on them saddens me.

Did She Ever Admit to Her BPD?

Did she ever admit to me that problems in her life are deeply connected to the traits of BPD? Sort of, but not really.

There was one occasion when we argued about her wanting me to curtail my behavior around a certain woman while we attended a social function. I told her I didn't appreciate her unfounded accusations and would not agree.

As we were about to mingle, she said, "I know I might have a problem that needs to be dealt with, but it's a bigger issue than I can handle right now. So, could you please just do what I'm asking to get through the party?"

That was it—her big admission. She never brought it up again or offered to address the problem that she "might have."

But that is typical of BP denial. In *Stop Walking on Eggshells*, the authors say:

> *So, the BP had destroyed a relationship? She moves on to the next one and the next one after that and so on and so forth.*

Like I stated early in the book, nearly all of a BP's self-destructive actions can be boiled down to one statement: "Don't leave me." A small amendment would be, "That way I can leave you first." The authors of *Stop Walking on Eggshells* continue: "The fears are so vast, so encompassing, and so overwhelming that denial can be absolute."

Will We Ever See Each Other Again?

My new wife, Irene, has asked if I ever ponder reconnecting with Lyssa or how I would respond if she contacted me. I have a definite answer: I will not initiate communication with her.

It's clear that despite all my efforts, pretty much everything about me became a negative trigger for her. Even if she's doing great these days, hearing from me would likely do no good and might even do harm.

If she continued the same mindset as during much of our marriage, she still views me as a verbally abusive control freak. There's no upside to me reaching out, so it's best I leave the door closed.

What if I hear from her? Again, I'll take a pass. She had the tools and talent to achieve great things, and I hope she has done just that, but hearing from her directly serves no purpose in my life. We have completely released each other of any post-marriage obligation, and I like it that way.

Am I bitter? I have to admit that on rare occasions, the answer is yes. I wish I was 100% above such pettiness, but I can't always claim to be on the high road.

On a positive note, with all I've learned about BPD over the years, I am fully comfortable knowing it wasn't about me. **She would have treated any husband the exact same way.** I just happened to be the guy who didn't know enough to dodge the cookie-bullets.

Perhaps, it was even a good thing she was married to me instead a man who might have responded with a level of violence to put her in the hospital. As bad as things were, she could have found herself in a much more dangerous situation with someone else.

I've also come to accept that *she* is the true victim, not me. Her life was far more hellish than mine. I could usually find ways to escape the madness, even if only for brief periods. But she had to live within her splintered mind every minute of the day. Between the two of us, I certainly had the better deal.

However, there is one great regret I struggle with. I married Lyssa later in life and the range of years I spent with her are often considered "last call" for child-rearing. But because she was considerably younger, we agreed to delay starting a family.

In the ashes of our divorce, I promised myself to never again get involved with a woman outside my own age group. But already being in my mid-40s, that meant I was not going to father children of my own.

It's clear to me that having children with Lyssa would have been a lifetime battle of me constantly shielding them from the Crazy. But because of my choice to marry her and stay married as long as I did, my window for having offspring closed.

I am endlessly grateful to have gained step-kids in my new marriage, but my own bloodline will cease with me, and I consider that an affront to my ancestors. In my weak moments, I blame others for my poor choice to stay married to Lyssa. I'm working on it.

Let's Wrap This Up Shall We?

Life has been *amazingly positive* since I focused on me and the things I can control. I can't control people who freak out over seemingly bizarre, random events, but I can set boundaries and consequences. I can choose where to spend my time and who to spend it with.

I fully understand that the primary motivation of a BP is fear of abandonment and lacking self-image, and I will do everything I can to incorporate that awareness into how I respond to others in the future. But that doesn't mean I have to be a victim of disrespect. I allowed that in the past, and those days are over.

If someone around me is unable to curtail their personality disorder, BPD or otherwise, I understand what they're going through, but I don't have to accept it as normal in my life or anything I need to fix. I have come to love the expression, "Not my monkey, not my circus."

If a BP does x, I abso-freaking-lutely will do y, just the way I told them I would. I don't give a rip if they don't think it's fair. They don't have to keep me around if that's too much to accept.

They might spend tonight thinking I'm Satan, but I also know that tomorrow they'll likely think I'm a golden ray of sunshine. I'll come back later with open arms full of love. If they are still nasty to me, I'll love them anyway, but we won't be friends anymore.

It took an awful long time for this to sink in, but despite what society has taught me my whole life, it's not my job to go around rescuing all the ladies out there. Most of them are doing just fine on their own.

And I no longer worry about trying to make every person I meet content on the inside. I can smile and be thoughtful, but the heavy lifting is on them. The unfortunate truth is that there are a lot of people who are not comfortable being happy. I have to be okay with that. Such simple wisdom, but so hard to accept.

Hopefully you'll get there much sooner than I did.

◆ ◆ ◆

Other Borderline Personality Books from Robert Page
To visit my Amazon author page and see other titles about BPD, simply scan this QR code into your phone or device:

If you want to read more from me about BPD, here are other titles you should check out:

Could Your Spouse Have Borderline Personality Disorder? Understanding the Roses and Rage

This is a brief, down and dirty "street-guide" to the symptoms of BPD and how you can spot them in your own marriage. Most spouses of a BP have no idea what they are facing and that they are not alone in their struggle. Written *by* the spouse of a Borderline *for* the spouses of Borderlines. Book #1 in the *Roses to Rage BPD* series.

Married to Borderline Personality Disorder: *Your BPD Stories of Roses and Rage*

The only BPD book of its kind! Focused entirely on accounts shared by readers who have faced head-on living with a BP marriage. Learn from others who have already "been there—done that" presented in non-clinical and compassionate language. Book #3 in the *Roses to Rage BPD* series.

What's Your Story?

Join the Facebook support group, Roses and Rage: Spouses of Borderline Personality Disorder, to share your experiences. I would especially love to hear from spouses who have found ways to reduce the BPD problems in your relationship.

Pass It On!

If you enjoyed this book and found it useful, I'd be very grateful if you'd **post an honest review** at the Amazon website. The more reviews, the higher the chances that others who need the book will see it.

To leave a review, all you need to do is visit the book's Amazon page. While you're at the page, please "follow" me as an author so you'll be notified about future books.

Thank you for the support ~ Robert
In the eBook, you may click/tap here to leave a review.

OTHER RESOURCES

I am only presenting here resources that I have personally reviewed and found useful. I am happy to include additional resources in future printings and invite you to email me at robertpagewriter@gmail.com to make suggestions.

Arabi, Shahida. 2016. *Becoming the Narcissist's Nightmare: How to Devalue and Discard the Narcissist While Supplying Yourself.* CreateSpace Independent Publishing.

Borderline personality disorder. 2019. Article available online from the Mayo Clinic.

Borderline Personality Disorder. Undated public-domain pamphlet available from the National Institute of Mental Health.

DSM-IV and DSM-5 Criteria for the Personality Disorders. American Psychiatric Association.

Eddy, Bill. 2011. *Splitting: Protecting Yourself While Divorcing Someone with Borderline or Narcissistic Personality Disorder.* New Harbinger Publications.

Fjelstad, Margalis. 2014. *Stop Caretaking the Borderline or Narcissist: How to End the Drama and Get On with Life.* Rl Publishing.

Kreisman, Jerold, MD and Hal Straus. 2010. *I Hate You—Don't Leave Me: Understanding the Borderline Personality.* New York: Penguin Group.

Johnson, Merri Lisa. 2010. *Girl in Need of a Tourniquet: Memoir of a Borderline Personality.* Berkeley, CA: Seal Press.

Linehan, Marsha M. 2014. *DBT Training Skills Manuel,* 2nd ed. The Guilford Press.

Mason, Paul, MS and Randi Kreger. 2010. *Stop Walking on Eggshells: Taking Your Life Back When Someone You Care About Has Borderline Personality Disorder,* 2nd ed. Oakland, CA: New Harbinger Publications, Inc.

Stout, Martha. 2006. *The Sociopath Next Door.* Harmony Publishing.

ABOUT THE AUTHOR

Robert Page is a pen name. I hold a doctorate degree from a fully accredited state university and have published several #1 Amazon best-sellers in non-fiction. After a decade in academia, I returned to my home-state roots to work in a "dream job" with the support of my wife and family. Under my real name, I have written various accounts of my experience with BPD, but the details in this book are so revealing that it would be inappropriate for me to risk the anonymity of others against their wishes. Therefore, all the names (including the pets) and locations have been changed. Please follow my Amazon Author page for more information.

Made in the USA
Las Vegas, NV
02 November 2023

80128253R00095